Preface

This Activity Guide accompanies *Foundations of Restaurant Manage....... ......
Two*. It is designed to reinforce what you're learning in your textbook. You will find many different types of activities per chapter. To use the Activity Guide most effectively:

- Follow the directions. If you are instructed to research a topic on the Internet or in your text-book before completing the activity, be certain to gather all the information you need before you answer.

- Use your text to help you complete the activities.

- Check your answers for accuracy. If you have difficulty with answers, return to the text and read the information again.

- It is very difficult to "play catch-up." Complete the activities when they are assigned.

Note to the teacher: The answer key to the workbook is included on the Teacher's Resource CD. However, many of the activities in the workbook don't have "correct" answers, so student responses will vary.

Table of Contents

Chapter 5

Chapter 6

Chapter 7

Chapter 11

Chapter **1**

Activity 1.1
Test Your Breakfast Food and Sandwiches IQ

Directions

Mark each of the following statements related to breakfast food and sandwiches as either true (T) or false (F). For each false statement, rewrite it to make it a true statement.

Part 1—Dairy Products and Eggs

_____ 1. Pasteurization and homogenization are both terms that mean milk has been made safe to drink.

_____

_____

_____ 2. A person who is lactose intolerant has an allergy to milk.

_____

_____

_____ 3. Milk should be received and stored at temperatures of 41°F or lower.

_____

_____

_____ 4. Clarified butter is used in cooking because of its higher smoke point, which makes it less likely to burn when heated.

_____

_____

_____ 5. All cheeses are made up of equal parts water, fat, and protein, and the texture and flavor are determined by the geographic location of the cheese maker.

_____

_____

_____ 6. The egg is a complex food composed of the outer shell, albumen, and yolk.

_____

_____

_____ 7. The most commonly used size of egg in foodservice operations are large eggs (24 ounces per dozen).

_____

_____

_____ 8. Shell eggs are graded by the USDA as Grade AA, A, or B, and eggs look different depending on the grade.

_____

_____

Part 2—Breakfast Foods and Drinks

_____ 1. Crêpes are thin pancakes made from a batter that has a high egg content.

_____

_____

_____ 2. Bacon is approximately 30 percent fat and does not shrink much when cooking.

_____

_____

_____ 3. Hash is a short name for hash-browned potatoes, a popular breakfast item.

_____

_____

_____ 4. Grapefruit, served halved either raw or broiled with brown sugar, is a very popular breakfast fruit item.

_____

_____

_____ 5. Coffee is made from the bean of a tropical shrub.

_____

_____

_____ 6. When brewing coffee, it is important to begin with boiling water.

_____

_____

_____ 7. There are several varieties of tea that can be served, including black tea, green tea, and oolong tea.

_____

_____

_____ 8. Hot beverages, such as coffee, maintain their flavor well and can be kept in a serving pot for up to eight hours.

_____

_____

Part 3—Sandwiches

_____ 1. Sandwiches can be placed into one of two general categories: hot or cold.

_____

_____

_____ 2. The sandwich is said to have gotten its name from John Montagu, Fourth Earl of Sandwich.

_____

_____

_____ 3. A panini is a type of sandwich that can be made in a waffle iron.

_____

_____

_____ 4. Depending on where you live, this sandwich, which is served on a long roll with several types of meats, cheeses, and toppings such as lettuce, tomato, and onion, may be called a sub, hero, grinder, or hoagie.

_____

_____

_____ 5. A small open-faced sandwich served as an hors d'oeuvre is called a wrap sandwich.

_____

_____

_____ 6. *Mise en place* means to have everything together that will be needed for a particular item.

_____

_____

_____ 7. Spreads, such as mayonnaise, are used to add flavor and moisture to a sandwich.

_____

_____

_____ 8. Sandwich stations require large quantities of special equipment.

_____

_____

Activity 1.2
Crossword Puzzle—Dairy Products and Eggs

Directions

Complete the following statements, and then use the answers to complete the crossword puzzle.

ACROSS

2. This milk, _____, is often used in baking when richness and sweetness are needed.

4. A semi-soft mild cheese with a buttery flavor and a wax rind. _____

5. The process of putting eggs into cold water immediately after cooking to stop the cooking process. _____

9. This item is used to add flavor and richness to a dish and is made by mixing cream containing between 30 and 45 percent milkfat at a high speed. _____

11. An egg dish made by beating eggs and cooking them in a skillet with a filling. _____

13. A waxy substance found in certain foods such as meat, dairy products, or eggs. _____

14. A butter substitute that usually contains no milk products. _____

15. A type of butter used in cooking because it does not burn easily. _____

16. The process used to kill microorganisms in milk that can cause spoilage or disease. _____

DOWN

1. This egg weighs between 3½ to 5 pounds and is equal to two dozen chicken eggs. _____

2. The process of separating milk's solids from its liquid is called _____.

3. A type of baked egg. _____

6. A very hard ripened cheese that may take at least two years to ripen. _____

7. A savory egg custard baked in a crust. _____

8. This type of milk has a thick texture and a tangy acid taste. _____

10. Made from whole or skim milk, this is often used in baking and is made by removing all water from milk. _____

12. A small oven-proof, ceramic dish used to bake eggs. _____

13. The membranes that hold the egg yolk in place are called _____

www.CrosswordWeaver.com

Activity 1.3
Lab—Make Your Own Cheese

Directions

Some form of cheese is found in virtually all cultures. Cheese can be soft and gooey or hard and pungent. Cheese is made by separating milk solids from its liquid and then processing it in a variety of ways, depending on the type of cheese desired.

Objectives

After completing this lab activity, you should be able to:

- Apply effective *mise en place* through practice
- Demonstrate proper use of equipment and tools
- Follow basic food safety and sanitation guidelines
- Follow basic safety guidelines to avoid causing injury to self or others
- Prepare cheese

Directions

1. Review the recipe.
2. Perform *mise en place.*
3. Plan for any substitutions or additional ingredients you have been given.
4. Prepare the recipe.
5. Clean the area.

Basic Farmer's Cheese

Yield: approximately 1 lb

Measure	Ingredients
1 gal	Whole milk
Pinch	Salt
½ c	White vinegar

Directions

1. Pour the milk into a large pot.

2. Stir in a pinch of salt.

3. Gradually bring the milk to a boil, stirring occasionally to prevent the milk from burning.

4. When the milk begins to boil, check the temperature. Small bubbles will start to form along the edge of the pan and the temperature should be 190°F.

5. Stir in the white vinegar (or if you prefer, ¼ cup of fresh lemon juice).

6. Wait for the milk to curdle (5 to 10 minutes).

7. Line a colander with several layers of cheesecloth and pour the milk through the cheesecloth to catch the curds.

8. The product in the cheesecloth is your cheese. Wrap the cheesecloth around this and squeeze out any excess juice (whey).

9. Wrap the cheese in plastic and place in an airtight container in the refrigerator.

Note:

The liquid in the colander is whey and can be used in a soup or stew, or thrown away.

Variations

Add freshly chopped herbs to the cheese before wrapping in plastic and placing in the refrigerator.

Add fresh ground pepper or finely diced jalapeno peppers to the cheese to make a "hot" cheese.

Substitution

Substitute ¼–½ cup fresh lemon juice in place of the white vinegar.

Activity 1.4
Webquest—The Incredible Egg

Directions

You will be going on a Webquest, a virtual Easter egg hunt. Use the space below to answer the questions about the different egg sites that you will be visiting. You will be provided with the URLs for the Webquest, and you will need to provide detailed answers to the questions about each URL.

Egg Cookery

http://www.aeb.org/foodservice-professionals/recipes/featured-recipes

Visit the page for foodservice professionals and find three recipes. In the space provided, write down the name of the recipe, the number of servings, and a brief description of the item.

1. Breakfast sandwich

_____

_____

_____

_____

_____

_____

_____

2. Egg entrée

_____

_____

_____

_____

_____

_____

_____

3. School foodservice egg recipe

_____

_____

_____

_____

_____

_____

_____

Egg Safety

http://www.eggsafety.org/

Explore the egg safety site and answer the following questions using the space provided.

1. Explain how *Salmonella* spp. infects eggs and why you should be concerned.

_____

_____

_____

_____

_____

_____

_____

2. Describe the variations in an egg's color.

_____

_____

_____

_____

_____

_____

_____

_____

Specialty Eggs

http://www.aeb.org/foodservice-professionals/specialty-eggs

Learn more about several different specialty eggs and answer the following questions.

1. Compare an organic egg with a regular egg.

_____

_____

_____

_____

_____

_____

_____

2. Compare and contrast free-range eggs and cage-free eggs.

_____

_____

_____

_____

_____

_____

_____

Egg Products

http://www.aeb.org/food-manufacturers/overview

Explore this page and learn more about egg production, and then answer the following questions.

1. How many million cases of shell eggs were used in 2007 in the form of egg products?

_____

_____

_____

_____

_____

_____

2. In 1998, how many dozen total broken shell eggs were used compared to 2008?

_____

_____

_____

_____

_____

_____

_____

Incredible Edible Egg

http://www.incredibleegg.org/egg-facts/eggcyclopedia

Last stop: Visit the Eggcyclopedia, and research egg facts based on your initials. Share the results in the space provided below.

1. First Name Fact

_____

_____

_____

_____

_____

_____

_____

2. Last Name Fact

_____

_____

_____

_____

_____

_____

_____

Activity 1.5
Lab—Egg Cookery

Directions

Eggs are an excellent protein source and can be served for breakfast, lunch, or dinner. From a simple hard-boiled egg to an elaborate soufflé, the egg is a versatile ingredient.

Recipe Selection

- Scrambled Eggs with Cheese
- Vegetable Frittata
- Spinach Quiche
- Cheese Soufflé

Objectives

After completing this lab activity, you should be able to:

- Apply effective *mise en place* through practice
- Demonstrate proper use of equipment and tools
- Follow basic food safety and sanitation guidelines
- Follow basic safety guidelines to avoid causing injury to self or others
- Prepare and serve a variety of breakfast foods
- Know and be able to describe a number of egg preparations

Directions

1. Review the recipe you have been assigned.
2. Perform *mise en place.*
3. Plan for any substitutions or additional ingredients you have been given.
4. Prepare the recipe.
5. Clean the area.

Scrambled Eggs with Cheese

Yield: 1 serving   Serving Size: 1 oz

Measure	Ingredients
3	Eggs, whole, large
2 tbsp	Milk
¼ c	Sharp cheddar cheese, shredded
To taste	Salt and pepper
As needed	Chopped parsley for garnish

Directions

1. In a medium size bowl, crack the eggs. Check that no shells are in the bowl.

2. Add the milk and whisk the eggs and milk until they are blended together.

3. Use a large, non-stick skillet that has been lightly sprayed with cooking oil.

4. Pour the egg mixture into the skillet.

5. Cook the eggs over medium heat. When the edges start to harden, stir frequently with a spatula.

6. When the eggs are cooked almost all the way, turn the heat down to low.

7. Sprinkle the shredded cheese on top of the eggs, and continue stirring with the spatula.

8. Once the cheese has melted and the eggs are done, remove from heat.

9. Plate the eggs, and serve with your choice of breakfast meat and fruit garnish.

Vegetable Frittata

Yield: 6 servings

Measure	Ingredients
1 c	Broccoli, chopped
1	Red pepper, small dice (green pepper can be used instead)
1 tbsp	Olive oil
6 oz	Button mushrooms
1 clove	Fresh garlic, minced
2	Green onions, minced
1 small or ½ large	Green or yellow zucchini, sliced in half circles
6	Large shell eggs
⅓ cup	2% milk
To taste	Salt
To taste	Pepper
1 tbsp	Chives, chopped fine
¼ cup	Parmesan cheese, freshly grated
2 medium	Tomatoes, sliced thin

Directions

1. Preheat oven to 350°F.
2. Wash and trim broccoli.
3. Clean and slice mushrooms.
4. Clean and dice peppers.
5. In a large skillet, heat the olive oil and sauté the mushrooms over medium heat for approximately 10 minutes. While the mushrooms are cooking, mince the garlic and green onions and add to the mushrooms, cooking for an additional 2 to 3 minutes. Remove the mixture from the heat.
6. Cut the zucchini in half and then slice into small half circles.
7. In a large bowl, mix the eggs, milk, salt, pepper, and chives.
8. Add the broccoli, pepper, mushroom mixture, and zucchini.
9. Spray a 2-quart baking dish (11″ × 7.2″) with cooking spray.
10. Pour the egg and vegetable mixture into the dish.
11. Slice the tomatoes and layer on the egg mixture. Sprinkle with Parmesan cheese and bake in the oven for 30–35 minutes until eggs are set and firm.
12. Cool before serving.

Note: If you prefer the cheese to be browned and melted, place under a broiler for 2–3 minutes.

Substitutions

Use a softer cheese such as mozzarella in place of the Parmesan.

Spinach Quiche

Yield: 8 servings

Measure	Ingredients
1	Pie shell, 9″, unbaked
1	Egg white, lightly beaten
6 tbsp (¾ stick)	Butter or margarine
½ c	Onion, chopped fine
10 oz	Spinach (frozen, thawed, drained, chopped)
2 tbsp	Parsley
4 slices	Bacon, crisp
1½ cups (6 oz)	Swiss cheese, grated
4	Eggs
1 c	Light cream
¼ tsp	Salt
⅛ tsp	Nutmeg
To taste	Pepper

Directions

1. Brush the inside of the pie shell with the egg white, and refrigerate.

2. In a medium skillet, melt the butter and then sauté the onions until golden, approximately 5 minutes.

3. Chop the parsley.

4. Drain the spinach.

5. Add the spinach and parsley to the onions and mix well.

6. Remove from the heat and pour into a large bowl.

7. Preheat oven to 375°F.

8. In a small skillet, cook the bacon until crisp. Drain and crumble into small pieces.

9. Remove the pie crust from the refrigerator, and sprinkle the bacon pieces on the bottom.

10. Sprinkle the Swiss cheese over the bacon. Set aside.

11. In a medium bowl, beat the eggs with the cream, salt, nutmeg, and pepper until combined but not foamy. Mix the egg mixture with the spinach mixture.

12. Pour the egg-and-spinach mixture over the cheese and bacon in the pie crust.

13. Bake for 45–50 minutes on the bottom rack of the oven.

14. Let cool for at least 10 minutes on a wire rack before serving.

Cheese Soufflé

Yield: 6 servings

Measure	Ingredients
6 tbsp	Butter or margarine
½ cup	All-purpose flour
Dash	Red pepper, ground
1½ c	Whole milk
3 c	Cheddar cheese, shredded
6	Egg yolks, beaten
6	Egg whites, stiffly beaten

Directions

1. Make a basic white sauce by mixing the butter, flour, milk, and red pepper in a saucepan.

2. Add the shredded cheese and cook until the milk and cheese have melted.

3. Gradually add the egg yolks.

4. Cool the mixture and fold in the stiffly beaten egg whites.

5. Pour into a greased soufflé dish.

6. Set the soufflé dish in a pan of water, and bake at 350°F for 45 minutes.

Activity 1.6
Lab—Rise and Shine

Directions

Breakfast is widely considered the most important meal of the day. A balanced breakfast can include a variety of food—including cheese, eggs, and potatoes—as well as the traditional pancakes, waffles, or cereal. The addition of meat, fruit, or toast completes the meal and gives you the energy to put your best food forward!

Recipe Selection

- French Toast
- Cheese Strata
- Pancakes
- Corned Beef Hash with Poached Eggs

Objectives

After completing this lab activity, you should be able to:

- Apply effective *mise en place* through practice
- Demonstrate proper use of equipment and tools
- Follow basic food safety and sanitation guidelines
- Follow basic safety guidelines to avoid causing injury to self or others
- Prepare and serve a variety of breakfast foods

Directions

1. Review the recipe you have been assigned.
2. Perform *mise en place.*
3. Plan for any substitutions or additional ingredients you have been given.
4. Prepare the recipe.
5. Clean the area.

French Toast

Yield: 10 servings   Serving Size: 3 slices

Measure	Ingredients
30 slices	Bread, such as Challah or brioche (¼″ to ½″ thick)
32 fl oz	Milk
8	Eggs
2 oz (¼ c + 1½ tsp)	Sugar
Pinch	Cinnamon, ground
Pinch	Nutmeg, ground
To taste	Salt
3 fl oz	Butter, melted, or vegetable oil

Directions

1. Lay the slices of bread in a single layer on sheet pans, and allow to dry overnight.
2. Combine the milk, eggs, sugar, cinnamon, nutmeg, and salt.
3. Mix well with a whisk until smooth.
4. Refrigerate until needed.
5. Heat a skillet or non-stick pan over medium heat.
6. Brush the skillet or pan with a small amount of butter or vegetable oil.
7. Dip the bread slices into the batter, coating them evenly.
8. Cook the slices on 1 side until evenly browned.
9. Turn the bread and brown on the other side.
10. Serve at once on heated plates.

Note:

Dust with a light coating of confectioner's (powdered) sugar, and serve with warm maple syrup.

Cheese Strata

Yield: 6 servings

Measure	Ingredients
8 slices	Bread, day-old
8 oz	Cheese, Swiss, American, or cheddar
4	Eggs
2½ c	Milk
1 oz	Onions, small dice
1 clove	Garlic, minced
½ tsp	Mustard
1½ tsp	Salt
Pinch	Pepper
As needed	Paprika

Directions

1. Trim crust from bread and cut slices in half diagonally.

2. Cover the bottom of a 9″ × 9″ × 2″–inch baking pan with remaining bread and trimmings.

3. Place cheese slices over bread in pan and arrange the 8 triangles, in 2 rows, over the cheese.

4. Whip eggs. Add milk, onions, garlic, mustard, salt, and pepper; mix.

5. Ladle mixture over the bread and cheese and sprinkle with paprika.

6. Cover and chill for 4 hours or overnight.

7. At service time, bake uncovered in a 325°F oven for 1 hour 15 minutes.

8. To check for doneness, insert a knife near the center. If it comes out clean, the strata is cooked. Let sit for a few minutes before serving.

© Michael Zema, FMP/CCE. Used with permission.

Pancakes

Yield: approximately 16 servings (will vary based on size)

Measure	Ingredients
2 c	All-purpose flour, sifted
3 tsp	Baking powder
1 tsp	Salt
2 tbsp	Sugar
1	Egg
1½ c	Milk
3 tbsp	Oil
½ tsp	Vanilla extract

Directions

1. Mix dry ingredients together.
2. Gently stir in egg, milk, and oil.
3. Heat a medium-size skillet.
4. Add a small portion of oil or non-stick food spray.
5. Pour batter into skillet (approximately 1 ounce).
6. Brown on 1 side. (Pancakes are browning when bubbles begin to form around the edges.)
7. Flip the pancake over and continue browning.
8. Garnish with confectioner's (powdered) sugar. Serve with butter pats and warm syrup.

Variations

Add ½ cup of chocolate chips to the batter for chocolate chip pancakes.

Add ½–¾ cup fresh blueberries or frozen and drained blueberries for blueberry pancakes.

Add 2 medium mashed bananas for banana pancakes.

Corned Beef Hash with Poached Eggs

Yield: 12 servings

Measure	Ingredients
2 lb, 8 oz	Potatoes
2 lb	Onions, minced
½ c	Oil
1 lb, 8 oz	Cooked corned beef
5 tbsp	Herbs (mixture of rosemary, chives, thyme)
8 oz	Butter
To taste	Salt
To taste	Black pepper
12	Eggs, large
2 tbsp	Chopped chives or parsley for garnish

Directions

1. Steam the potatoes. Allow them to cool, and then cut into a medium dice.

2. Sauté the onions and potatoes until lightly browned. Set aside.

3. Cut the corned beef into ¼″ strips. Set aside.

4. Using a large skillet, melt the butter over medium heat, being careful not to burn it. Stir in the onions, potatoes, and herbs; sauté for approximately 2 minutes, until the potatoes are warm throughout but not soggy.

5. Gently stir in the corned beef, and sauté an additional 2 minutes. Season with salt and pepper.

6. Remove the potato and beef mixture from the heat and keep warm.

7. Poach eggs in small batches until egg whites are set and yolks are no longer runny (but not hard). Remove the eggs from the poaching water, and keep warm.

8. Place approximately ½ cup of the beef and potato hash mixture on a plate. Top with a poached egg.

9. Sprinkle fresh chives or parsley on top for a garnish.

Note:

Directions for Poaching an Egg:

1. Combine 1 cup water, a pinch of salt, and a dash of vinegar in a shallow skillet or pan, and bring to a boil.

2. Break the egg(s) into a clean cup, and slide the egg(s) carefully into the poaching water. Cook until the whites are set and opaque.

3. Remove the egg(s) from the water with a slotted spoon, and blot them on a paper towel.

Activity 1.7
Research/Presentation—Coffee, Tea, or Energy Drinks

Directions

You have been asked by a local health club to research the benefits of coffee, tea, and energy drinks. The club is considering adding breakfast to the food offerings provided to members and wants to determine the health benefits of offering several different types of caffeinated beverages. For the presentation, the owner of the health club would like to know the following:

1. What is the difference between coffee, tea, and popular energy drinks in terms of flavor and caffeine content?

2. What health benefits are offered from drinking coffee? Tea? Energy drinks?

3. What are at least two potential negatives that result from drinking coffee? Tea? Energy drinks?

4. What are the different types of coffee, tea, or energy drinks that are available?

Specific Information

Select either coffee, tea, or energy drinks to do more detailed research on. The owner would like to know the following:

1. What is the best way to prepare and serve the beverage you selected?

2. What are some of the rituals or traditions associated with the beverage you selected?

3. If selecting energy drinks, what is the difference between an energy drink and soda?

The research should be done using information provided in the text, other books, magazines, and material found on the Internet. The material should be presented in a written brief with a short four- to five-slide PowerPoint or other electronic presentation to support the report.

Take your notes in the space below.

_____

_____

_____

_____

_____

_____

_____

_____

Activity 1.8
Lab—Sandwiches

Directions

Hot, cold, simple, or complex, sandwiches can be satisfying and a convenient meal for people of all ages. There is no limit to the different sandwiches you can create once you understand the three basic components of sandwiches—bread, spread, and filling. Let's experiment!

Recipe Selection

- Chicken Salad Sandwich
- Tuna Melt
- Club Sandwich
- Grilled Cheese with Bacon and Tomato
- Tuna Salad Sandwich

Objectives

After completing this lab activity you should be able to:

- Apply effective *mise en place* through practice
- Demonstrate proper use of equipment and tools
- Follow basic food safety and sanitation guidelines
- Follow basic safety guidelines to avoid causing injury to self and others
- Prepare common sandwich spreads and fillings
- Demonstrate preparation of several types of sandwiches

Directions

1. Review the recipe you have been assigned.
2. Perform *mise en place*.
3. Plan for any substitutions or additional instructions you have been given.
4. Prepare the recipe.
5. Clean the area.

Chicken Salad Sandwich

Yield: 6 servings

Measure	Ingredients
1 lb	Cooked chicken, small dice
3 oz	Celery, small dice
1 oz	Onion, small dice
1 c	Mayonnaise
1 tsp	Lemon juice
To taste	Salt
To taste	Pepper
6 leaves	Lettuce
12 slices	Bread
6 slices	Tomato, optional
As needed	Alfalfa sprouts, optional

Directions

1. Combine cooked chicken with celery, onions, mayonnaise, and lemon juice.

2. Adjust seasonings with salt and pepper. Cover and refrigerate at least 4-6 hours to blend flavors.

3. At service time, place a lettuce leaf on each of 6 slices of bread. Top with 2-3 oz of chicken salad and sliced tomatoes and alfalfa sprouts, if desired. Place second slice of bread on top.

4. Slice sandwiches in half diagonally and serve.

Tuna Melt

Yield: 10 servings

Measure	Ingredients
1 lb, 8 oz	Albacore tuna, canned and drained (in water)
10 fl oz	Mayonnaise
4 oz (¾ c)	Celery, minced
4 oz (⅔ c)	Onions, minced
To taste	Garlic powder (optional)
2 tsp	Worcestershire sauce, or as needed
To taste	Salt and white pepper, freshly ground
To taste	Dry mustard
20	English muffins, sliced in half crosswise
10 oz	Cheddar cheese, sliced
4 oz (½ c)	Butter, as needed

Directions

1. Flake the tuna, and place it in a large bowl.

2. Add the mayonnaise, celery, and onions. Mix well.

3. Season with garlic powder (if using), Worcestershire sauce, salt, pepper, and mustard to taste.

4. Place 4 oz tuna salad on a slice of muffin.

5. Top with cheese and another slice of muffin.

6. Brush the outside of the muffins lightly with butter.

7. Griddle over medium heat, until golden brown on both sides.

Note:

Garnish with salad greens.

Club Sandwich

Yield: 10 servings Serving size: 1 sandwich each

Measure	Ingredients
20 slices	Whole wheat bread, lightly toasted
10 slices	White bread, lightly toasted
¼ cup (approx)	Mayonnaise
20 leaves	Lettuce
20 slices	Tomato
30 strips	Bacon, cooked crisp
20 oz	Sliced turkey

Directions

Note: You will be making one sandwich at a time

1. Place 3 slices of toast (2 slices of whole wheat and 1 slice of white bread) on a clean work space.

2. Spread a thin layer of mayonnaise on the top of each piece of toast.

3. The first slice of toast will be the base of the sandwich. Place 1 lettuce leaf, 2 tomato slices, and 3 pieces of crisp bacon on this.

4. Put the second piece of toast on top of the bottom layer, mayonnaise side up.

5. Place the turkey on top and then add 1 leaf of lettuce.

6. Add the third piece of toast, mayonnaise side facing down.

7. Use 4 frill toothpicks to hold the sandwich together. Place a frill toothpick in each side.

8. Cut the sandwich into 4 triangles (cutting from corner to corner on each side).

9. Serve on a plate with the points of each triangle facing up.

10. The plate may be garnished with potato chips, fries, dill pickle spears, cole slaw, or other garnish.

Grilled Cheese with Bacon and Tomato

Yield: 4 servings   Serving size: 1 sandwich

Measure	Ingredients
8 slices	Bacon, crisp
¼ c	Butter, softened
8 slices	White, wheat, or French bread
8 slices	White cheddar cheese or American cheese
8 slices	Tomato

Directions

1. Heat a large skillet over medium heat.

2. Lightly spread butter on each piece of bread (butter side up).

3. Place 4 slices of bread (butter side down) in the skillet.

4. Place a slice of cheese, 2 slices of bacon, and 2 slices of tomato on each piece of bread.

5. Add another slice of cheese on top of the tomato.

6. Cover with a slice of bread (butter side up).

7. Grill sandwiches until golden brown and cheese is melting.

Note:

For variety, use two different types of cheese on each sandwich. Other cheeses that work well include: mozzarella, muenster, or Swiss.

Tuna Salad Sandwich

Yield: 6 servings   Serving size: 1 sandwich

Measure	Ingredients
1 lb	Flaked tuna
3 oz	Celery, small dice
1 oz	Onion, small dice
1 c	Mayonnaise
1 tsp	Lemon Juice
¼ tsp	Fresh tarragon, chopped
1	Hard-cooked egg, chopped medium
To taste	Salt
To taste	Pepper
6 leaves	Lettuce
12 slices	Bread
As needed	Tomatoes (sliced)
As needed	Red onions (sliced)

Directions

1. Combine tuna, celery, onions, mayonnaise, lemon juice, tarragon, and hard-cooked egg. Mix well.

2. Adjust seasoning to taste with salt and pepper.

3. Refrigerate for 1 hour before service.

4. At service time, place a lettuce leaf on each of 6 slices of bread.

5. Spread with 3-4 oz of tuna salad and top with second slice of bread.

6. Slice in half diagonally and serve open-faced.

7. If desired, garnish with tomatoes and/or red onions.

Activity 1.9
Pizza Time

Directions

You have been asked to design a pizza buffet by the owners of a sports center. They will be hosting a competition for 120 cheerleaders and will end the first night of activities with a pizza buffet. Plan for each attendee to eat at least four slices of pizza. The owner would also like all the pizzas to be homemade and there needs to be a variety, as some of the cheerleaders are vegetarian, some prefer meat, and there are about 10 percent who are lactose intolerant. All of the pizzas should be made from scratch on site.

In order to successfully complete this project you will need to complete the following four tasks:

1. Determine the menu. In order to meet the dietary requirements you will need at least three, but not more than six, different types of pizza. Use the space provided to write down your pizza ideas.

2. Find recipes for the pizzas you selected for the menu. You can find these by reading cookbooks, cooking magazines, and visiting recipe sites online. Using separate pieces of paper or a word processing program, write down the recipes. Be sure to include the source.

3. Create a supply list of all the ingredients needed in the proper amount. This should be created on a spreadsheet. Consider creating a separate page in the spreadsheet for each type of pizza.

4. Create a shopping list of ingredients for the chef and a printed copy of the menu, with descriptions of each pizza for the guests. Write down your final ingredient list and your menus with descriptions.

Take your notes in the space below. Use additional sheets of paper, poster board, or your computer to create your final menu and ingredient list.

_____

_____

_____

_____

_____

_____

_____

_____

_____

_____

_____

_____

Activity 10.1
Design a Sandwich Shop

Directions

You have been hired by the Chamber of Commerce to design a new sandwich shop for the downtown area. The shop will seat 40 diners and will primarily focus on "to-go" orders and catering. The shop will be open for lunch and dinner. You have been asked to present a core menu and to design the front- and back-of-the-house areas following best practices for safety and sanitation.

When designing the sandwich shop, be sure to include the following:

- Dining area (include wall décor, tables, and lighting)
- Food-preparation area (determine if the guests can watch their sandwich being made or if sandwiches will be made in the kitchen and served)
- Ovens if bread will be baked fresh, or display racks if bread will be purchased from a bakery
- Sink and dishwashing area
- Refrigeration and storage
- Food preparation areas

Present your design to your classmates, and explain why you chose the concept you did.

Take your notes in the space below. Use a separate sheet of paper, poster board, or your computer to create your presentation.

Chapter **2**

Activity 2.1
Test Your Knowledge of Nutrition IQ

Directions

Mark each of the following statements related to nutrition as either true (T) or false (F). For each false statement, rewrite it to make it a true statement.

Part 1—The Basics of Nutrition

____ 1. Nutrition is the study of the components of food needed for the body to function.

_____

_____

____ 2. Malnutrition is the result of poor diet, generally caused by a lack of nutrients.

_____

_____

____ 3. There are six basic categories of nutrients that are required to maintain good health.

_____

_____

____ 4. Phytochemicals are the chemicals that give green, leafy vegetables their color.

_____

_____

____ 5. The unit of measure for energy, when discussing nutrition, is the kilocalorie, often referred to as a calorie.

_____

_____

___ 6. Carbohydrates are a poor source of energy for the body and primarily cause the body to store fat.

_____

_____

___ 7. Fiber is unique because it is found only in plant food and cannot be digested by people.

_____

_____

___ 8. There are 20 amino acids found in food and 12 of these are known as essential amino acids, which must be eaten weekly.

_____

_____

___ 9. Food additives are substances added to food as a result of the manufacturing process.

_____

_____

___ 10. A vegetarian is someone who consumes no meat, fish, or poultry products.

_____

_____

___ 11. LDL is often called "bad" cholesterol and is a result of eating foods with high levels of saturated fats and transfats.

_____

_____

___ 12. Malnutrition is responsible for causing many major diseases, including diabetes and obesity.

_____

_____

Part 2—Making Menu Items More Nutritious

_____ 1. One of the first steps in making sure menu items are nutritious takes place during the receiving process when deliveries are checked for freshness.

_____

_____

_____ 2. The FIFO system of rotating inventory is the least effective method for insuring product freshness.

_____

_____

_____ 3. Eating raw foods, especially fruits and vegetables, is always the most nutritious food option.

_____

_____

_____ 4. Proper cooking of foods ensures not only the safety of the diner but also a high quality, nutritious meal.

_____

_____

_____ 5. Batch cooking is a process used when large quantities of food are needed at one time.

_____

_____

_____ 6. There are several methods that can be used to make a dish healthier, including adding more fiber, fruits or vegetables, or reducing the fat content.

_____

_____

_____ 7. Kosher salt is often used in cooking because it is very fine and can be used in ice cream makers or as a bed for oysters on display.

_____

_____

_____ 8. Organic products have been grown without the use of pesticides or synthetic fertilizers.

_____

_____

_____ 9. A product that displays the USDA organic label has met specific government standards in terms of growing and handling of the product.

_____

_____

_____ 10. Genetically modified foods do not provide any nutritional benefits to consumers.

_____

_____

Activity 2.2
Crossword Puzzle—The ABCs of Nutrition

Directions

Complete the following statements, and then use the answers to finish the crossword puzzle.

ACROSS

4. Without proper _____ it is impossible for the body to function at its peak.

8. These fats are generally more saturated than liquid vegetable oils. _____

10. These blue nutrient chemicals are found in foods that are naturally purple in color. _____

14. This very important simple sugar is called _____ and is the body's primary source of energy.

15. A common starch is _____.

16. _____ are liquid at room temperature.

DOWN

1. An important hormone used to regulate sugar is _____

2. Another word for fat is _____ .

3. An example of a high-fiber food would be _____.

5. The energy released by some nutrients is measured in _____.

6. This is found only in plant foods and is essential for good health. _____

7. These are examples of complex carbohydrates. _____

9. The chemical process that causes unsaturated fats to spoil is called _____ .

11. Special chemical messengers that regulate different body functions are known as _____.

12. _____ are examples of simple carbohydrates.

13. Carbohydrates provide the body with _____.

www.CrosswordWeaver.com

Activity 2.3
Analysis—Nutrition Labels

Directions

Examine the nutrition labels provided to you in class, and then answer the following questions based on the information provided in the label.

1. Which food item has the fewest fat grams per serving?

2. Which food item has the highest percentage of fat per serving?

3. Which food item has the most milligrams of sodium per serving?

4. Which item has the most grams of protein per serving?

5. Which three or four items would you group together to make a healthy, balanced diet for an adult, based on the Recommended Dietary Allowances?

_____

_____

_____

_____

_____

6. Which item(s) would you recommend to a person who has to limit his or her intake of sodium?

_____

_____

_____

_____

_____

7. Which item(s) would you recommend to a person who has to limit his or her intake of fat?

_____

_____

_____

_____

_____

Activity 2.4
Healthy Diet—Menu Creation

Directions

You have been hired as a nutritional consultant for a local healthcare company to design and develop healthy-eating plans for several clients. Each client has a unique set of health challenges. In order to complete this project, three elements must be submitted to the client:

- A one-week menu that includes breakfast, lunch, dinner, and two healthy snacks per day

- Five recipes (at least one breakfast, one lunch, two dinner, and one snack)

- Tip sheet of why the items you selected for the menu will help them meet their nutrition goals

Use the calendar template provided in the workbook to write your menu, or use a calendar program found on-line or in your word processing software.

Use the space provided below or a word processing program to write the recipes and tip list.

_____

_____

_____

_____

_____

_____

_____

_____

_____

_____

_____

_____

_____

_____

_____

_____

_____

_____

Weekly Menu	Sunday	Monday	Tuesday	Wednesday	Thursday	Friday	Saturday
Breakfast							
Lunch							
Dinner							
Snack 1							
Snack 2							

Activity 2.5
Magazine Article—Debating Fats

Directions

You have been hired by a national family magazine to write a 200–250 word essay about the role that fat plays in the diet. In the essay, the editors would like you to discuss the following:

- Compare and contrast the different types of fat.
- What steps can be taken to reduce saturated fat in the diet?
- What are some foods that are lower in fat that can be substituted for high-fat foods while still being tasty and nutritious?

Bonus

Many times, the magazine will also publish a recipe to supplement the article, so include a favorite family-friendly, low-fat recipe with your essay.

Take your notes in the space below. Use additional sheets of paper or a word processing program to create your final essay.

Activity 2.6
Design a Magazine Ad

Directions

You have been hired by a local bottled water company to design a one-page ad for a local magazine. Working in teams, design the ad to promote either the importance of taking a multivitamin or proper hydration through drinking water. The ad should include the following components:

- Visuals (these can be drawn by hand, photographs, or clip art)
- Facts about the importance of vitamins or water in maintaining good health
- Benefits to using this product

Take your notes in the space below. Use a separate sheet of paper, poster board, or your computer to create your ad.

_____

_____

_____

_____

_____

_____

_____

_____

_____

_____

_____

_____

_____

_____

_____

_____

_____

_____

Activity 2.7
Research Paper—Nutrition-Related Diseases

Directions

Create a PowerPoint presentation or poster describing a disease or illness. Choose one from the following list of diseases or illnesses:

- Diabetes
- Heart disease
- Obesity
- Osteoporosis
- Kidney disease

Include the following points in your presentation:

1. Number of Americans suffering or thought to be suffering from this type of disease/illness
2. Whether any of these illnesses are more prevalent based on gender, age, race, or geographic location and, if so, discuss the implications
3. Changes that can be made to the diet to minimize or prevent this illness
4. Consequences of letting the illness go untreated
5. An action plan to make people more aware of this illness and methods of prevention through diet changes

Be sure to include resources from at least three different sites, one of which should be an online journal or Web site devoted to the disease/illness that you selected.

Take your notes in the space below. Use your computer or a separate sheet of paper to create your presentation.

_____

_____

_____

_____

_____

_____

_____

_____

_____

_____

Activity 2.8
Lab—Heart-Healthy Cooking

Directions

More diners are requesting heart-healthy or low-fat options when dining out. In order to meet the demands of customers, it is important to understand how to make a nutritious and healthy dish.

Recipe Selection

- Cucumber-pineapple Salad
- Beef and Bean Chili
- Poached Chicken
- Ratatouille with Chicken

Objectives

After completing this lab activity, you should be able to:

- Apply effective *mise en place* through practice
- Demonstrate proper use of equipment and tools
- Follow basic food safety and sanitation guidelines
- Follow basic safety guidelines to avoid causing injury to self or others
- Prepare and serve a variety of heart-healthy foods

Directions

1. Review the recipe you have been assigned.
2. Perform *mise en place.*
3. Plan for any substitutions or additional ingredients you have been given.
4. Prepare the recipe.
5. Clean the area.

Cucumber-pineapple Salad

Yield: 4 servings

U.S. Measure	Ingredients
¼ cup	Sugar
⅔ c	Rice wine vinegar
2 tbsp	Water
1 c	Pineapple, fresh, peeled, cored, and cut into ¼″ cubes
1 large	Cucumber, peeled and thinly sliced
1 large	Carrot, peeled and julienned
⅓ cup	Red onion, thinly sliced
4 c	Mixed greens, washed and torn
1 tbsp	Sesame seeds, toasted

Directions

1. In a medium saucepan, combine the sugar, rice wine vinegar, and water. Bring to a boil.

2. Stir constantly, until reduced to a syrup, approximately ½ cup should remain. (This will take about 5 minutes.)

3. Pour the syrup into a large bowl and place in the refrigerator to cool.

4. Once the syrup has cooled, add the pineapple pieces, cover, and return to the refrigerator for one hour.

5. Add the cucumber, carrots, and red onions to the pineapple mixture. Toss until all ingredients are combined.

6. Place 1 cup of mixed greens on a plate, and top with the pineapple mixture.

7. Sprinkle 1 teaspoon of toasted sesame seeds on top.

8. Serve immediately.

Beef and Bean Chili

Yield: 4–5 servings   Serving Size: 8 oz

Measure	Ingredients
1½ lb	Ground beef, 95% lean
3 tsp	Vegetable oil
1 tsp	Garlic, minced
1 small	Onion, chopped fine
¾ tsp	Chili powder
½	Green pepper, chopped fine
1 large	Tomatoes, chopped
1 tsp	Oregano
¼ tsp	Cumin
1 c	Kidney beans, no salt if possible

Directions

1. In a large skillet, heat the vegetable oil and add the garlic and onion. Sauté until golden brown.

2. Add the ground beef to the onion-and-garlic mixture, and cook until brown.

3. Drain the beef.

4. Add the chili powder, pepper, tomatoes, oregano, cumin, and kidney beans. Simmer for 30 minutes, stirring occasionally.

5. Serve in soup bowls, and garnish with low-fat sour cream, and no-salt crackers.

Variations

Substitute 1 pound lean beef stew meat for the ground beef. If using stew meat, cut into 1″ cubes that are trimmed of fat. Use an additional 1½ tablespoon of vegetable oil to brown the meat. After the meat is browned, simmer with 2 cups of water in a covered saucepan for about 1 hour or until meat is tender, and then follow steps above.

Poached Chicken

Yield: 4–6 servings

Measure	Ingredients:
2½ lb	Chicken, or 4 boneless chicken breasts
1	Onion
1	Carrot
1 stalk	Celery
4 sprigs	Parsley
3 sprigs	Fresh thyme or ¼ tsp dried thyme
1 each	Bay leaf
1 tbsp	Tarragon
2 qt	Chicken stock, homemade is best
½ tsp	Salt
⅛ tsp	Fresh ground pepper

Directions

1. Cut chicken into 8 pieces using the 8-way method, remove skin. If using chicken breast, remove skin and bones.

2. Peel and cut onion into sections.

3. Peel and cut carrot on the bias into 1½″ slices.

4. Wash and cut celery stalk into 2 pieces.

4. Place parsley, thyme, and bay leaf on one-half of celery, cover with the other half so they fit together. Tie celery together with twine making a bouquet garni.

5. In a stockpot put chicken, onion, carrot slices, bouquet garni, tarragon, and stock.

6. Bring the stock to a boil and immediately lower the temperature so the stock is at a simmer.

7. Add salt and pepper to season. Important: If using canned stock or broth, reduce the salt by at least half.

8. Cover the stockpot and cook about 15–25 minutes, check the temperature of the chicken for 165°F. (Remember there will be hold-over cooking so the chicken will continue to cook after you remove it from the heat.)

9. Remove the chicken from the stock. You can reduce the stock and serve with the chicken or you can make a sauce with the chicken stock.

10. Serve the chicken with the carrot and onion, garnished with fresh tarragon.

Ratatouille with Chicken

Yield: 4 servings   Serving Size: 1½ cups

Measure	Ingredients
1 tbsp	Vegetable oil
4	Chicken breasts, boneless, skinless, cut in 1″ cubes
2 medium	Zucchini, unpeeled, thinly sliced
1	Eggplant, small, peeled, cut into 1″ cubes
1	Green pepper, large dice
½ lb	Button mushrooms, sliced
1 (16 oz) can	Whole tomatoes, cut
1 clove	Garlic, minced
1½ tsp	Basil, dried
1 tbsp	Fresh parsley, minced
To taste	Pepper

Directions

1. Heat oil in a large non-stick skillet. Add chicken, and sauté for approximately 3 minutes until lightly brown and thoroughly cooked.

2. Add the zucchini, eggplant, onion, green pepper, and mushrooms. Cook over low heat for approximately 15 minutes, stirring occasionally.

3. Add tomatoes, garlic, basil, parsley, and pepper. Continue cooking for approximately 5 minutes until chicken and eggplant are tender. Stir occasionally.

4. Serve with rice garnished with zucchini flower or tomato rose.

Activity 2.9
Lab—Recipe Substitutions

Directions

Many diners and home cooks are looking for tasty alternatives to high-fat and high-calorie foods. In this lab, you will prepare two versions of the same dish: one following the traditional recipe and one using substitutions to lower the fat or calories.

Recipe Selection

- Chocolate Cupcakes
- Blueberry Muffins
- Brownies

Objectives

After completing this lab activity, you should be able to:

- Apply effective *mise en place* through practice
- Demonstrate proper use of equipment and tools
- Follow basic food safety and sanitation guidelines
- Follow basic safety guidelines to avoid causing injury to self or others
- Prepare and serve a low fat alternative item

Directions

1. Review the recipe you have been assigned.
2. Perform *mise en place.*
3. Plan for any substitutions or additional ingredients you have been given.
4. Prepare the recipe.
5. Clean the area.

Cupcakes from a Boxed Mix vs. Diet Soda Cupcakes

Chocolate Cupcakes from a Mix

Yield: 24 cupcakes

Measure	Ingredients
1 box	Prepared chocolate cake mix
1 c	Water
⅓ c	Vegetable oil
3	Whole eggs
1 can	Prepared frosting

Directions

1. Prepare cupcakes according to package directions.
2. When completely cool, frost using a can of prepared frosting.

Diet Soda Cupcakes

Yield: 24 cupcakes

Measure	Ingredients
1 box	Prepared chocolate cake mix
12 oz	Diet soda
12 oz	Low-fat whipped topping

Directions

1. Prepare cupcakes according to package directions substituting diet soda for water, eggs, and oil.
2. When completely cool, frost with low-fat whipped topping.
3. Garnish with fresh strawberries.

Regular Blueberry Muffin vs. Low-Fat/Low-Sugar Blueberry Muffin

Regular Blueberry Muffin

Yield: 12 muffins

Measure	Ingredients
1½ c	All-purpose flour
¾ c	Sugar, white
½ tsp	Salt
2 tsp	Baking powder
⅓ c	Vegetable oil
1	Egg, whole
⅓ c	Milk, whole
1 c	Blueberries, fresh
½ c	Sugar, white
⅓ c	All–purpose flour
¼ c	Butter, cubed
1½ tsp	Cinnamon, ground

Directions

1. Preheat oven to 400°F. Line a cupcake pan with muffin cups or lightly grease.

2. Combine 1½ cups flour, ¾ cup sugar, salt, and baking powder in a medium bowl.

3. In a small bowl, add the vegetable oil, egg, and milk.

4. Combine the liquids with the flour mixture.

5. Gently fold in blueberries.

6. Fill muffin cups to the top.

7. To make crumb topping, combine ½ cup sugar, ⅓ cup flour, ¼ cup butter, and cinnamon. Fix with fork until crumbly. Sprinkle over muffins.

8. Bake for 20–25 minutes, or until golden brown.

Low-Fat/Low-Sugar Blueberry Muffin Converted from Blueberry Muffin Recipe

Yield: 12 muffins

Measure	Ingredients
1½ c	All-purpose flour
¾ c	Splenda®
½ tsp	Salt
2 tsp	Baking powder
⅓ c	Vegetable oil
¼ c	Egg substitute (such as Egg Beaters®)
⅓ c	Milk, skim
1 c	Blueberries, fresh

Directions

1. Preheat oven to 400°F. Line a cupcake pan with muffin cups or lightly grease.

2. Combine 1½ cups flour, ¾ cup Splenda®, salt, and baking powder in a medium bowl.

3. In a small bowl, add the vegetable oil, egg, and milk.

4. Combine the liquids with the flour mixture.

5. Gently fold in blueberries.

6. Fill muffin cups to the top.

7. Bake for 20–25 minutes, or until golden brown.

Traditional Brownie

Yield: 16 brownies

Measure	Ingredients
½ c	Butter
1 c	Sugar, white
2	Eggs, whole
1 tsp	Vanilla extract
⅓ c	Cocoa powder, unsweetened
½ c	All-purpose flour
¼ tsp	Salt
¼ tsp	Baking powder

Directions

1. Preheat oven to 350°F.
2. Lightly grease and flour an 8″ square pan.
3. In a large saucepan, melt ½ cup butter. Remove from heat, and stir in sugar, eggs, and vanilla.
4. Beat in cocoa powder, flour, salt, and baking powder.
5. Using a spatula, spread into prepared pan.
6. Bake for 25–30 minutes. Brownies are done when cake tester comes out clean. Be careful not to overbake.
7. Place on rack to cool.

Brownie—Low-fat version

Yield: 16 brownies

Measure	Ingredients
½ c	Applesauce, unsweetened
1 c	Splenda®
½ c	Egg substitute
1 tsp	Vanilla extract
⅓ c	Cocoa powder, unsweetened
½ c	All-purpose flour
¼ tsp	Salt
¼ tsp	Baking powder

Directions

1. Preheat oven to 350°F.

2. Lightly grease and flour an 8″ square pan.

3. In a medium bowl, combine applesauce, Splenda®, eggs, and vanilla.

4. Beat in cocoa powder, flour, salt, and baking powder.

5. Using a spatula, spread into prepared pan.

6. Bake for 25–30 minutes. Brownies are done when cake tester comes out clean. Be careful not to overbake.

7. Place on rack to cool.

Activity 2.10
Presentation—Should GMOs Be Regulated?

Directions

You have been asked by a local service club to give a two- to three-minute presentation on genetically modified organisms (GMOs). The club has asked for two speakers, one to present the pros of GMO's and one to present the cons. During the presentation you must include the following elements:

- What is a GMO?

- Examples of foods that have been (or have not been) modified

- Benefits/risks to eating GMO food

- What can be done to encourage/prevent increased use of GMOs

Create your presentation using presentation software (such as PowerPoint) or create a poster to support your view. In the presentation, be sure to include graphics, charts, and key definitions.

Take your notes in the space below. Use a separate sheet of paper, poster board, or your computer to create your poster.

_____

_____

_____

_____

_____

_____

_____

_____

_____

_____

_____

_____

_____

_____

_____

_____

_____

Chapter **3**

Activity 3.1
Test Your Knowledge of Cost Control IQ

Directions

Mark each of the following statements related to cost control as either true (T) or false (F). For each false statement, rewrite it to make it a true statement.

Part 1—Introduction to Cost Control

_____ 1. In order for any business to be successful, costs must be higher than revenue.

_____

_____

_____ 2. Controllable costs are those items that are subject to change and can be controlled by a business to some extent.

_____

_____

_____ 3. Variable costs are ones that increase or decrease in direct proportion to sales.

_____

_____

_____ 4. An operating budget is an unchanging financial plan.

_____

_____

_____ 5. A forecast is used to predict future sales during a set time period.

_____

_____

_____ 6. A profit-and-loss report lists sales and income for a specific time period and can be used to compare the performance of an operation over time.

_____

_____

_____ 7. Full-line suppliers are companies that carry only one brand of a product.

_____

_____

Part 2—Controlling Food Costs

_____ 1. The flow of food process is a seven-step process that begins with preparing product.

_____

_____

_____ 2. Food cost is the actual dollar value of food used by an operation during a certain time period, and it includes not only food sold, but food that is spoiled or wasted.

_____

_____

_____ 3. Total food cost percentage is a fixed cost that will not vary depending on sales or product purchased.

_____

_____

_____ 4. Standard recipes are used to maintain consistency in product appearance and cost.

_____

_____

_____ 5. The As-purchased method of costing uses the cost of an ingredient after it has been trimmed and cleaned.

_____

_____

_____ 6. The food production chart is a tool used by the kitchen to show how much product should be produced during a specific meal period.

_____

_____

_____ 7. The menu is the main sales tool in a restaurant, and a number of methods can be used to price menu items, including average check, straight markup, and food cost percentage.

_____

_____

Part 3—Controlling Labor Costs

_____ 1. Labor is considered a semivariable cost because some positions are fixed costs, such as a manager, while others vary based on business.

_____

_____

_____ 2. Several factors can play a role in controlling labor costs, including the cost of food, advertising, and employee morale.

_____

_____

_____ 3. Employee turnover refers to the number of employees who are hired to fill a position during a year's time.

_____

_____

_____ 4. The restaurant and foodservice industry is the 4th largest employer in the country, employing nearly 20 million people.

_____

_____

_____ 5. A master schedule is a template used to assist in the scheduling process and lists the number of employees needed to staff the operation based on projected sales.

_____

_____

_____ 6. A contingency plan is something that can be used when business doesn't run as planned, for example, during a power outage or bad weather.

_____

_____

_____ 7. Cross-training employees is not considered good business due to the time and effort it takes for limited results.

_____

_____

Part 4— Controlling Quality Standards

_____ 1. The intended use for a product must be clearly defined in order for the operation's quality standards to be met.

_____

_____

_____ 2. The best time to receive deliveries is during the lunch hour, when the operation is fully staffed and food can be put away quickly.

_____

_____

_____ 3. Well-defined receiving procedures are created so that an operation receives the highest-quality product when it is needed.

_____

_____

_____ 4. Monitoring production, to ensure standard recipes are used properly, is one way to be sure quality standards are being met.

_____

_____

_____ 5. A physical inventory is conducted once a month and is based on reviewing the invoices and receipts for all deliveries.

_____

_____

_____ 6. According to the National Restaurant Association, 10 percent of all inventory shortages are due to accounting errors.

_____

_____

Activity 3.2
Crossword Puzzle—Cost Control

Directions

Complete the following statements, and then use the answers to complete the crossword puzzle.

ACROSS

1. The standard _____ is the exact amount that one portion of food costs when prepared according to the standard recipe.

4. An _____ budget is a financial plan created for a specific time period.

5. A _____ is a chart that shows the employees' names, dates, and times they are needed at work.

8. The _____ is a seven-step process that begins with purchasing and ends with service.

9. A recipe _____ is the process of determining how many portions a recipe will produce.

10. A document from a vendor that lists the items purchased, the date of purchase, and the sales price is called an _____.

11. The _____ _____ _____ allows operators to run historical reports and production reports based on data entered into them.

DOWN

2. _____ costs are fixed costs and include items such as insurance, utilities, and rent or lease costs.

3. A _____ cost is one that can change based on sales.

6. The actual dollar value of the food used by an operation during a specific period is referred to as _____.

7. _____ sales per customer are computed by dividing the total amount of sales by the total number of customers.

www.CrosswordWeaver.com

Activity 3.3
Profit-and-Loss Statement Information

Directions

Part 1

Below is a list of the information typically found on the profit-and-loss statement (P&L). Using the letters A through E, indicate the order in which the information appears on a P&L. (For example, the information that appears first, or at the top of the statement, would be indicated by the letter A.)

Information	Order on P&L Statement
1. Cost of Sales	
2. Net Income	
3. Sales	
4. Expenses	
5. Income	

Part 2

Answer the following questions related to the P&L:

1. Net income is also referred to as what? _____

2. The profit and loss statement is also referred to as an _____

3. How often are income statements (or P&Ls) prepared? _____

_____

_____

4. What must an operation do in order to be profitable? What can an operation do to help ensure its success?

_____

_____

_____

Bonus Question

5. Frankie's is an Italian restaurant and banquet hall with total annual revenue of $436,050. The banquet department is responsible for bringing in 44 percent of the operation's total revenue and has total annual expenses of $76,300. Based on this information, calculate the revenue generated by the banquet department last year (in dollars).

_____

_____

Activity 3.4
Costing and Pricing—Gazpacho

Directions

Part 1

Calculate the cost for each of the ingredients in the gazpacho recipe below. Use the table to record your calculations. When you have completed the table, calculate the following:

Cost per ounce: _____

Cost per serving: _____

Suggested selling price per serving at 27 percent food cost percentage: _____

Gazpacho

Yield: 20 servings   Serving Size: 6 oz

Ingredient	Amount	Cost of Ingredient	Cost
Tomatoes	6 ¾ lb	$2.45 lb	
Cucumbers	64 oz	$9.50, 15-lb box	
Onions	24 oz	$0.65 lb	
Green bell peppers	1½ lb	$3.18 lb	
Crushed garlic	1 oz	$3.15 lb	
Breadcrumbs	32 oz	$4.29, 3-lb box	
Tomato juice	1¼ qt	$6.25, ½ gal	
Red wine vinegar	8 oz	$2.75 pt	
Olive oil	16 oz	$1.25 c	
Salt	To taste	$0.15 per recipe	
Pepper	To taste	$0.15 recipe	
Lemon juice	5 tbsp	$0.25 recipe	
Total			

Part 2

Convert the gazpacho recipe so that it yields 120, 4-ounce servings. Use the table below to record your calculations. Then, calculate the answers to the following based on the converted recipe.

Cost per ounce: _____

Cost per serving: _____

Suggested selling price per serving at 27 percent food cost percentage: _____

Gazpacho

Yield: 120 servings   Serving Size: 4 oz

Ingredient	Amount	Cost of Ingredient	Cost
Tomatoes	27 lb	$2.45 lb	
Cucumbers	16 lb	$9.50, 15-lb box	
Onions	6 lb	$0.65 lb	
Green bell peppers	6 lb	$3.18 lb	
Crushed garlic	4 oz	$3.15 lb	
Breadcrumbs	8 lb	$4.29, 3-lb box	
Tomato juice	1¼ qt	$6.25, ½ gal	
Red wine vinegar	1 qt	$2.75 pt	
Olive oil	2 qt	$1.25 c	
Salt	To taste	$0.60 recipe	
Pepper	To taste	$0.60 recipe	
Lemon juice	¼ c	$1.25 recipe	
Total			

Activity 3.5
Case Study—The Cost Control Caper

Directions

Read the following case study. When you are finished reading, answer the questions that follow the case study. Record your answers in the space provided.

Case Study

The Chocolate Mountain is a new, casual restaurant that specializes in chocolate treats and also offers a few simple sandwiches. While the operation has quickly developed a reputation for serving delectable desserts and is always busy, the manager is mystified. The manager has hired you to help solve the mystery.

Here is what you already know about The Chocolate Mountain:

- Customer counts are increasing, but revenues are decreasing.

- Some servers are complaining about the small tips. Many customers are requesting that the servers themselves add 15 percent to the bill as the gratuity. Some of the servers are simply giving back exact change anyway.

- Both the sandwich chef and the confection chef have complained to the manager that they can't read the servers' handwriting and are making mistakes on the orders. As a result, some ice cream treats and sandwiches have had to be remade.

- The Chocolate Mountain opened in the month of September with $1,700 in its food inventory and closed with $1,950. September purchases totaled $8,500, and food sales for the month were $14,400.

Case Study Questions

1. What was the food cost percentage for The Chocolate Mountain in September?

_____

_____

2. Is this an acceptable food cost percentage in the restaurant and foodservice industry?

_____

_____

3. Analyze the information, and identify ways to control costs and and improve the food cost percentage.

_____

_____

4. How can the management of The Chocolate Mountain improve employee job satisfaction?

_____

_____

Activity 3.6
Lab—Yield Test

Directions

In this activity, you will be preparing carrots, potatoes, and apples for cooking. You will be assessed on your accuracy and neatness.

Using the chart provided, record the starting amount of product used, the amount of finished product, and the amount of trim or waste.

Item	Starting Amount	Ending Amount	Loss (%)
Carrots			
Potatoes			
Apples			

Your goal for each item is as follows:

- Carrots—1 cup shredded
- Potatoes—1 cup diced
- Apple—1 cup chopped

Activity 3.7
Practice—Menu Markup

Directions

Use the information provided on the menu below to calculate your answers.

Easy Street Café
Menu

Salads—served with choice of dressing and rolls

Fresh Garden Salad $4.95

Cobb Salad $5.95

Taco Salad $5.95

Side Salad $2.95

Sandwiches—served with choice of fries, onion rings, or coleslaw

Turkey Sandwich $5.25

Tuna Salad Sandwich $5.75

Ham and Cheese Sandwich $6.25

Grilled Cheese Sandwich $4.75

Sides

Onion Rings $1.25

Cup of Soup $2.00

French Fries $2.25

Fresh Fruit $2.00

Desserts

Ice Cream Bars $2.25

Apple Pie..$2.00, with Ice Cream .. $3.00

Scoop of Ice Cream $2.50

Chocolate Cake $1.75

Beverages

Soda $1.00

Coffee or Tea $1.50

Milk $1.25

Orange Juice $1.50

1. David orders a ham and cheese sandwich, onion rings, and tea. He has a text message on his phone for a 10 percent discount. If the tax is 6.5 percent, what will David's total bill be?

_____

2. Ms. Peterson orders a grilled cheese sandwich with fresh fruit and a soda. Kellie orders a taco salad and milk. Whose order costs more?

_____

3. Mr. Jones wants to treat his son and four friends to ice cream bars. If he gives the counter server $13.00 and tells her to "keep the change," how much change will the server get? (Include 6.5 percent in the price of the ice cream for tax.)

_____

4. The manager of the Easy Street Café opens the shop at 11 a.m. on Friday. Immediately she notices that the freezer is not running—it is broken. There were two unopened cases of ice cream bars in the freezer that thawed and must be thrown away. If there are 24 bars in a case, what is the revenue loss from the ruined ice cream bars?

_____

5. If the purchase price for each case of ice cream bars is $15.50, what is the dollar value of the inventory lost?

_____

6. What is the food cost per ice cream bar?

_____

7. If the Easy Street Café used a straight 75 percent markup pricing method, what would the price be for one ice cream bar?

_____

Activity 3.8
Case Study—Standard Portion Costs

Directions

Read the case study below. Then, calculate the answer to the problems that follow the case study.

Case Study

Andrea, the manager of a coffee shop in a suburban mall, purchases pies for her restaurant from a well-known, local bakery. For service, Andrea cuts each fruit pie into six slices and cuts each cream pie into eight slices. The pie prices listed on Andrea's menu are $2.09 for a slice of fruit pie and $2.59 for a piece of cream pie.

Below is a copy of the invoice for pies that Andrea ordered from the bakery during the month of April.

> ## Invoice
> ## Sweet Treats Bakery
>
> 125 Riverside Drive
>
> Precious, TN 37222
>
> Date: May 1, 2012   Invoice #: A245
>
> Terms: Net 30 days
>
> Sold to: Andrea's Café   P.O. Box 1456
>
> 123 Main Street   Contact: Andrea Smith
>
> Precious, TN 37222   Phone: 615-555-1234

Item	Quantity	Unit Cost	Cost
Apple pie (whole)	5	$3.49	$17.45
Cherry pie (whole)	5	$3.79	$18.95
Peach pie (whole)	7	$3.99	$27.93
Chocolate cream pie (whole)	4	$4.29	$17.16
Coconut cream pie (whole)	4	$4.69	$18.76
		Total	$100.25

1. Calculate Andrea's standard portion cost for one slice of apple pie. _____

2. Calculate Andrea's standard portion cost for one piece of coconut cream pie. _____

3. Calculate Andrea's average portion cost for pie in the entire month of April. _____

4. If a whole peach pie weights 1 pound, calculate Andrea's cost per ounce for peach pie. _____

5. If a whole peach pie weighs 1 pound, calculate the price of each slice of pie. _____

Activity 3.9
Calculating Selling Prices

Directions

Part 1

Identify each of the menu-pricing methods described on the left. Letters may be used more than once.

1. Multiply raw food cost by a predetermined fraction	A.	Food cost percentage method
2. Gives an idea of the range of prices on a menu	B.	Average check method
3. Item cost ÷ Food cost percentage = price	C.	Contribution margin method
4. Yields a desired profit at an expected level of sales volume	D.	Straight markup method
5. Total revenue divided by number of seats, average seat turnover, and days open in 1 year		
6. Minimum acceptable dollar amount would be met (if sales volume matched forecasted sales and costs were kept strictly under control)		

Part 2

Using the information provided, calculate the answers to the following problems:

1. The food cost for a chicken sandwich is $1.94. If the manager desires a food cost percentage of 26 percent, calculate the sandwich's selling price (rounded up to the nearest $0.05).

2. The food cost for a complete spaghetti dinner is $1.67. On the menu, the selling price is listed as $7.00. Calculate the food cost percentage for the dinner.

3. Calculate the selling price for the spaghetti dinner listed in question two if the manager were to use a straight 200 percent markup.

4. Calculate the selling price for the spaghetti dinner listed in question two if the manager were to use the contribution margin method, and the average contribution was $2.82 per customer?

5. Calculate the food cost percentage for the spaghetti dinner in question four?

Activity 3.10
Poster/Presentation—Implementing Quality Standards in the Kitchen

Directions

Create a poster/presentation that can be displayed in the kitchen to remind the staff of the importance of purchasing, receiving, and storage in maintaining quality standards in the kitchen.

This information can be displayed as a poster, electronic presentation, or some other type of visual. Incorporate a combination of images and text and decide on three key elements for purchasing, receiving, and storing. Share the presentation with your classmates.

Take your notes in the space below. Use a separate sheet of paper, poster board, or your computer to create your poster.

Chapter **4**

Activity 4.1
Test Your Knowledge of Salads and Garnishing IQ

Directions
Mark each of the following statements related to salads and garnishing as either true (T) or false (F). For each false statement, rewrite it to make it a true statement.

Part 1—Salads

_____ 1. The three keys to ensuring a quality salad are use high quality iceberg lettuce, blend the ingredients together, and make sure the salad focuses on two main ingredients.

_____

_____

_____ 2. The four basic parts to any salad are the base, body, garnish, and dressing.

_____

_____

_____ 3. The base of the salad is usually a layer of salad greens that line the plate or bowl.

_____

_____

_____ 4. Salad dressings are used to hold the salad together and traditionally are mayonnaise based.

_____

_____

_____ 5. A bound salad is primarily made from raw ingredients, such as vegetables or fruit.

_____

_____

_____ 6. Salads once were served only as a first course but now can be used in five different ways during service.

_____

_____

_____ 7. An intermezzo salad is meant to cleanse the palate after a rich dinner and before the dessert or cheese course.

_____

_____

Part 2—Salad Dressings and Dips

_____ 1. The type of salad dressing used should complement the ingredients of the salad, for example, delicate ingredients will taste better with a lighter dressing.

_____

_____

_____ 2. Vinaigrette dressings are made from three parts oil and one part vinegar, and then shaken together.

_____

_____

_____ 3. An emulsion is a permanent blending of dissimilar ingredients.

_____

_____

_____ 4. It's important to apply mayonnaise-based dressing as long before service as possible so flavors can blend together.

_____

_____

_____ 5. Hummus is a dip made with avocado, Serrano peppers, and garlic.

_____

_____

_____ 6. Dips can be served hot or cold and should complement the food items they are served with.

_____

_____

Part 3—Garnishes

_____ 1. A proper garnish complements the main dish by adding both eye appeal and flavor.

_____

_____

_____ 2. A garnish is often an afterthought or extra part of the dish.

_____

_____

_____ 3. When arranging food on the plate, it is important to keep food off the rim and arrange the plate in unity.

_____

_____

_____ 4. It is important for servers to know all ingredients used in a dish, in case a guest has a food allergy.

_____

_____

_____ 5. Napping is a technique used in baking desserts that allows the dough to rest before garnishing.

_____

_____

_____ 6. A gougères is a small finger-sized pastry that can be used to garnish soups.

_____

_____

Activity 4.2
Crossword Puzzle—Salad Time

Directions

Complete the following statements, and then use the answers to complete the crossword puzzle.

ACROSS

2. _____ can be used alone or with other greens and must be washed thoroughly before serving.

7. _____ is also known as chicory and has a slightly bitter flavor.

9. _____ contains oxalic acid and has a slightly acidic and bitter flavor.

10. A _____ salad is served as an appetizer before the main meal and is often smaller in size.

DOWN

1. The _____ enhances the appearance of the salad and complements the overall taste.

3. _____ is a type of green that has a pungent, peppery flavor and can be used as a garnish.

4. A _____ salad is a green salad where the ingredients are mixed together.

5. _____ is a salad green that has a pungent and distinct flavor.

6. The _____ of the salad consists of the main ingredients.

8. A _____ salad is usually sweet and may contain fruit, nuts, and whipped cream.

www.CrosswordWeaver.com

Activity 4.3
Lab—Lunch and Dinner Salads

Directions

Salads can appear in any course of a meal. In this lab, we are focusing on entrée salads that can be the entire meal. Salads are a good source of vegetables, fiber, and often protein. Now that you've learned the four parts of a salad—base, body, garnish, and dressing—let's practice!

Recipe Selection

- Caesar Salad
- Couscous Salad
- Spinach Salad
- Chef's Salad

Objectives

After completing this lab activity, you should be able to:

- Apply effective *mise en place* through practice
- Demonstrate proper use of equipment and tools
- Follow basic food safety and sanitation guidelines
- Follow basic safety guidelines to avoid causing injury to self or others
- Prepare and serve a variety of salads

Directions

1. Review the recipe you have been assigned.
2. Perform *mise en place.*
3. Plan for any substitutions or additional ingredients you have been given.
4. Prepare the recipe.
5. Clean the area.

Caesar Salad

Yield: 2 servings

Measure	Ingredients
To taste	Salt
2 small or 1 large	Garlic clove
2	Anchovy fillets
1	Egg yolk, pasteurized
½	Lemon
1 tsp	Dijon mustard
¼ c	Parmesan cheese
½ c	Olive oil
½ head	Romaine lettuce, inner leaves
½ c	Croutons

Directions

1. Place 2 salad plates in the freezer before service.
2. Lightly salt the bowl and add garlic. Using 2 forks, mash into a paste.
3. Add anchovies to the paste and mash.
4. Add egg yolk, and whip.
5. Add a small squeeze of lemon juice, and continue to whip.
6. Add mustard and half of the Parmesan cheese, and whip.
7. Slowly add the oil, and whip to form an emulsion. Add remaining lemon juice to adjust taste.
8. Add the romaine lettuce and toss (away from guests, toward yourself).
9. Add remainder of cheese and croutons. Save some for top of salad.
10. Place on chilled plates. Offer anchovy garnish and fresh ground pepper.

© Michael Zema, FMP/CCE. Used with permission.

Couscous Salad

Yield: 1 serving

Measure	Ingredients
3 oz	Couscous
3 oz	Boiling water or stock
½	Red pepper, medium dice
½	Green pepper, medium dice
1 bunch	Green onions, small dice
2 oz	Black olives, pitted, sliced
3 oz	Red onion, julienne

Vinaigrette Dressing

Measure	Ingredients
1½ oz	Fresh orange, grapefruit, lime, or lemon juice
1 oz	Chicken stock
1 oz	Rice wine vinegar
½ tsp	Roasted garlic, minced
½ tsp	Salt
½ tsp	Black pepper
1 tsp	Fresh oregano, finely chopped
1 tsp	Fresh thyme, finely chopped
1½ oz	Salad oil
½ oz	Waffle syrup

Directions

1. Add couscous to boiling liquid; cover, and let stand about 5 minutes; cool.
2. Combine couscous with peppers, green onions, olives, and red onions.
3. In a separate bowl, whisk together vinaigrette ingredients.
4. Combine salad with vinaigrette, and chill before service.
5. Serve on a chilled plate.

© Michael Zema, FMP/CCE. Used with permission.

Spinach Salad

Yield: 6 servings

Measure	Ingredients
1 lb	Fresh spinach, chopped
¼ c	Green onions, sliced
3 slices	Bacon, medium dice
1 tbsp	Wine vinegar
2 tsp	Lemon juice
1 clove	Roasted garlic, minced
½ tsp	Sugar
¼ tsp	Salt
3 oz	Fresh button mushrooms, sliced
To taste	Ground black pepper
1	Hard cooked egg, chopped
As needed	Croutons
As needed	Red pepper rings

Directions

1. Place spinach and green onions in a large, stainless steel bowl.

2. Sauté bacon until crisp. Add vinegar, lemon juice, garlic, sugar, and salt. Do not drain bacon drippings.

3. Simmer for 2–3 minutes, and remove from heat.

4. Pour pan dressing over spinach and onions. Add mushrooms and pepper, and toss lightly.

5. Place salad on serving dish, and sprinkle with egg.

6. Top with croutons, and garnish with red pepper, if desired.

© **Michael Zema, FMP/CCE. Used with permission.**

Chef's Salad

Yield: 4 servings

Measure	Ingredients
8 c	Salad greens, torn into bite-sized pieces. Iceberg, spinach, romaine, etc. Use your favorite combinations.
1 c	Ham, cooked, julienne
1 c	Turkey breast, cooked, julienne
½ c	Green onion, chopped fine
½ c	Carrots, shredded
1 c	Cherry tomatoes, halved
½ c	Swiss cheese, julienne
½ c	Cheddar cheese, julienne
2	Eggs, hard-boiled, peeled, sliced
¼ c	Bacon bits
To taste	Salad dressing

Directions

1. Wash and spin salad greens.

2. Tear greens into bite-sized pieces, and place in large bowl.

3. Toss the greens with the remaining ingredients, except salad dressing. Reserve small portion of ham, turkey, and cheese for garnish.

4. Place into serving bowls or salad plates, and dress the salad. Garnish with ham, turkey, cheese, and slices of hardboiled egg.

Activity 4.4
Lab—Side Salads

Directions

Let's continue exploring the versatile salad. In addition to being served as an entrée, there are a wide variety of salads that can be served as a side dish or accompaniment to round out the meal. Today, we'll explore some of the more frequently ordered side salads.

Recipe Selection

- Pasta Salad
- Creamy (or American) Potato Salad
- German Potato Salad
- Cole Slaw

Objectives

After completing this lab activity, you should be able to:

- Apply effective *mise en place* through practice
- Demonstrate proper use of equipment and tools
- Follow basic food safety and sanitation guidelines
- Follow basic safety guidelines to avoid causing injury to self or others
- Prepare and serve a variety of side or accompaniment salads

Directions

1. Review the recipe you have been assigned.
2. Perform *mise en place.*
3. Plan for any substitutions or additional ingredients you have been given.
4. Prepare the recipe.
5. Clean the area.

Pasta Salad

Yield: 6 servings

Measure	Ingredients
64 oz	Water
¼ tsp	Salt
¼ tbsp	Oil
8 oz	Pasta
2 oz	Asparagus tips, cooked
2 oz	Broccoli florets, cooked
2 oz	Cauliflower florets, cooked
2 oz	Carrots, small dice, cooked
2 oz	Sugar snap peas, cooked
8 oz	Basic vinaigrette
To taste	Salt
To taste	Pepper

Directions

1. Combine water with salt and oil, and bring to rolling boil.

2. Add pasta, and cook until al dente, not overcooking. Drain and cool.

3. Steam the asparagus, broccoli, cauliflower, and carrots in a steamer until tender crisp (al dente).

4. Place pasta in a large, stainless steel bowl, and add asparagus, broccoli, cauliflower, carrots, and peas. Toss lightly.

5. Add vinaigrette, and toss gently to combine.

6. Taste, and adjust flavor with salt and pepper.

© Michael Zema, FMP/CCE. Used with permission.

Creamy (American) Potato Salad

Yield: 6 servings

Measure	Ingredients
1½ lb	New potatoes
1 c	Celery, small dice
½ c	Onions, brunoise
1 clove	Garlic, minced
¼ c	Sweet pickle relish
1 c	Mayonnaise
2 tsp	Sugar
2 tsp	Celery seed
2 tsp	Vinegar
2 tsp	Dijon mustard
1 tsp	Salt
2	Hard boiled eggs, chopped
¼	Red or green pepper, julienne (garnish)

Directions

1. Cook potatoes until tender, but not overcooked (about 30 minutes in boiling liquid). Cool, and cut into large dice.

2. Combine potatoes, celery, onions, garlic, and relish in a large, stainless steel bowl.

3. Combine mayonnaise, sugar, celery seed, vinegar, mustard, and salt in a separate bowl.

4. Add dressing to potato mixture, and toss lightly to coat.

5. Add half the crumbled eggs, and continue to toss.

6. Cover and chill.

7. At service time, sprinkle remaining eggs and peppers (if desired) on top for garnish.

8. Serve on a chilled plate.

© **Michael Zema, FMP/CCE. Used with permission.**

German Potato Salad

Yield: 8 servings

Measure	Ingredients
5 lb	All-purpose potatoes
4 oz	Bacon, diced
8 oz	Onions, diced
4 oz	White wine vinegar
4 oz	Salad oil
To taste	Salt
To taste	Pepper
2 tbsp	Prepared mustard
16 oz	Hot chicken stock
2 oz	Chives, snipped

Directions

1. Cook, peel, and thinly slice potatoes.

2. Sauté bacon until nearly cooked. Add onions, and sweat, draining off excess liquid.

3. Combine vinegar, oil, salt, pepper, mustard, stock, and chives to make dressing.

4. Combine dressing, bacon, and onion mixture with sliced potatoes.

5. Serve salad warm.

© **Michael Zema, FMP/CCE. Used with permission.**

Creamy Coleslaw

Yield: 6 servings

Measure	Ingredients
3 oz	Mayonnaise
2 oz	Light cream
½ oz	Cider vinegar
½ oz	Sugar
½ tsp	White pepper
½ tsp	Celery seed
To taste	Salt
1 lb	EP green cabbage, shredded

Directions

1. Combine mayonnaise, cream, vinegar, sugar, pepper, celery seed, and salt to make dressing.

2. Toss cabbage with dressing, coating well.

3. Adjust flavor, if necessary.

4. Serve on a chilled plate.

© Michael Zema, FMP/CCE. Used with permission.

Activity 4.5
Webquest—Salad Anyone?

Directions

You will be participating in a Webquest, a virtual Easter egg hunt. Use the space provided below to answer questions from the different sites you will be visiting as you learn more about salads. You will be provided with the URLs for this Webquest and will need to provide the answers.

Lettuce

Fresh lettuce is a treat and some restaurants may choose to grow their own. Explore this site from the University of Illinois, and answer the following questions: http://urbanext.illinois.edu/veggies/lettuce.cfm

1. What are the five distinct types of lettuce?

_____

_____

_____

_____

_____

2. Except for iceberg lettuce, what are the main vitamins and minerals provided by lettuce?

_____

_____

_____

_____

_____

Food Facts

Food Facts and trivia are a fun way to test the knowledge of your staff and also a way to add a little extra something to dull dinner parties. Answer the following lettuce trivia questions from the Food Reference article on lettuce: http://www.foodreference.com/html/flettuce.html

1. Why did the ancient Greeks and Romans serve lettuce at the end of the meal?

_____

_____

_____

_____

2. According to the USDA, how much of the country's lettuce is produced in California (as of 2006)?

_____

_____

_____

_____

_____

3. Perhaps you have heard of the Waldorf salad, a classic made with apples, celery, walnuts, and raisins. But do you know the history behind the salad? Read all about it here: http://www.kitchenproject.com/history/Waldorf_Salad.htm. Describe the history of the salad.

_____

_____

_____

_____

_____

Gelatin Salads

Salads don't just need to be made from lettuce and vegetables. Gelatin salads have been popular for many years. Spend some time exploring the Jell-o site, and then answer these questions about these refreshing dessert salads: http://brands.kraftfoods.com/jello/explore/history/

1. When did congealed salads first become popular?

_____

_____

_____

_____

_____

2. Visit the recipes' section of the site, and find two Jell-o salad recipes, one for spring/summer and one for fall/holiday. Be sure to include the name of the salad you selected.

_____

_____

_____

_____

_____

Activity 4.6
Lab—Dressings and Dips

Directions

Salad dressings and dips add zest and flavor to vegetables and other accompaniments. A well-made dressing or dip can enhance the diner's experience. Explore some of these classics.

Recipe Selection

- Basic Vinaigrette
- Basic Mayonnaise
- Caesar Dressing
- Roquefort Dressing
- Raspberry Vinaigrette
- Guacamole
- Hummus

Objectives

After completing this lab activity, you should be able to:

- Apply effective *mise en place* through practice
- Demonstrate proper use of equipment and tools
- Follow basic food safety and sanitation guidelines
- Follow basic safety guidelines to avoid causing injury to self or others
- Prepare and serve a variety of salad dressings

Directions

1. Review the recipe you have been assigned.
2. Perform *mise en place.*
3. Plan for any substitutions or additional ingredients you have been given.
4. Prepare the recipe.
5. Present each dressing on a buffet.
6. Using a lettuce leaf or small piece of bread, taste each dressing, and record your observations regarding taste, texture, mouth feel, heaviness, etc.
7. Clean the area.

Basic Vinaigrette

Yield: 1 quart

Measure	Ingredients
24 oz	Olive, salad, sesame, vegetable, or flavored oil
8 oz	White, red, tarragon, cider, or other flavor vinegar
2 tbsp	Fresh dill, chives, or tarragon, chopped
½ tsp	Dry mustard
To taste	Salt
To taste	Pepper
To taste	Sugar (optional)

Directions

1. Combine all ingredients.

2. Blend well and adjust seasoning.

3. Marinate for 1 hour.

Note:

An oil-to-vinegar ration of 3:1 is a good formula for making vinaigrettes.

© **Michael Zema, FMP/CCE. Used with permission.**

Basic Mayonnaise

Yield: 12 ounces

Measure	Ingredients
1	Egg yolk
¼ oz	Wine vinegar
¼ oz	White stock
½ tsp	Dry mustard
8 oz	Vegetable, salad, olive, peanut, or other flavored oil
To taste	Lemon juice
To taste	Salt
To taste	Pepper

Directions

1. Combine egg yolk, vinegar, stock, and mustard in a stainless steel bowl. Mix ingredients well with a whip until slightly foamy.

2. Add oil slowly, while constantly beating mixture. Whip until all the oil is incorporated and the mayonnaise is thick.

3. Adjust flavor with lemon juice, salt, and pepper.

4. Refrigerate until service time.

Note:

An egg yolk-to-oil ratio of 1:8 is standard for most mayonnaise recipes.

Food Safety Note:

Food containing eggs that receive little or no cooking should be prepared with great care. Follow the directions precisely, and monitor temperatures using a thermometer. Many jurisdictions now require operators to post a notice to consumers when raw eggs are used as an ingredient in these types of recipes. The use of pasteurized eggs might be a safer alternative.

© **Michael Zema, FMP/CCE. Used with permission.**

Caesar Dressing

Yield: 32 ounces

Measure	Ingredients
3 oz	Anchovy fillets
½ oz	Prepared mustard
2–3 cloves	Garlic
1 tbsp	Worcestershire sauce
6 oz	Red wine vinegar
1 tsp	Ground black pepper
2 tbsp	Fresh lemon juice
2 oz	Parmesan cheese, freshly grated
½ tsp	Hot sauce
18 oz	Olive oil

Directions

1. Combine all ingredients except olive oil and lettuce in a blender or food processor, and blend for 10 seconds.

2. With blender or processor running, slowly add olive oil and process until all is incorporated.

© **Michael Zema, FMP/CCE. Used with permission.**

Roquefort Dressing

Yield: 1 pint

Measure	Ingredients
4 oz	Mayonnaise
½ oz	Red wine vinegar
4 oz	Sour cream
2 oz	Buttermilk
½ tsp	Roasted garlic, chopped
½ tsp	Worcestershire sauce
To taste	Hot pepper sauce
To taste	Pepper
6 oz	Roquefort cheese, crumbled

Directions

1. Combine all ingredients except cheese. Mix well.

2. Marinate for 1 hour, if possible.

3. At service time, add crumbled cheese, and blend.

© **Michael Zema, FMP/CCE. Used with permission.**

Raspberry Vinaigrette

Yield: 32 ounces

Measure	Ingredients
1	Whole egg
2 oz	Raspberry vinegar
1 tbsp	Dry mustard
4 oz	Raspberries, fresh
3 oz	Honey
24 oz	Vegetable oil
To taste	Salt
To taste	White pepper

Directions

1. Combine egg, vinegar, mustard, raspberries, and honey.

2. Slowly whisk in oil in a thin stream to emulsify.

3. Adjust seasoning to taste.

Food Safety Note:

Food containing eggs that receive little or no cooking should be prepared with great care. Follow the directions precisely, and monitor temperatures using a thermometer. Many jurisdictions now require operators to post a notice to consumers when raw eggs are used as an ingredient in these types of recipes. The use of pasteurized eggs might be a safer alternative.

© **Michael Zema, FMP/CCE. Used with permission.**

Guacamole

Yield: ½ pound

Measure	Ingredients
1	Fresh avocado
1	Shallot, minced
1 tsp	Cilantro, finely chopped
½ tbsp	Fresh lime juice
1 tsp	Fresh lemon juice
½ tsp	Jalapeño pepper, minced
¼ tsp	Garlic, mashed to a paste
2 oz	Tomatoes, diced (optional)

Directions

1. Combine all ingredients, and mash to a smooth paste with a fork.

2. Serve immediately or refrigerate.

© **Michael Zema, FMP/CCE. Used with permission.**

Hummus

Yield: 2 cups

Measure	Ingredients
15 oz	Garbanzo beans (canned)
2 oz	Jalapeño pepper, sliced
½ tsp	Cumin, ground
2 tbsp	Fresh lemon juice
3 cloves	Garlic, minced
½	Red bell pepper, cut in rings (optional garnish)

Directions

1. Drain the garbanzo beans and reserve the liquid.

2. In a blender or food processor, combine garbanzo beans, pepper, cumin, lemon juice, garlic, and 1 tablespoon of the bean liquid.

3. Blend until smooth.

4. Garnish with rings of red bell pepper.

Activity 4.7
Comparing Fresh and Premade Dips and Dressings

Directions

In this activity you will be comparing freshly made dips and dressings to their store-bought counterparts.

Part 1

Prepare one dip or dressing, and then create a chart and record nutritional values, taste, texture, mouth appeal, flavor, etc., of the freshly made item compared with the same premade item.

Take your notes in the space below. Use a separate sheet of paper, poster board, or your computer to create your chart.

_____

_____

_____

_____

_____

_____

_____

_____

_____

_____

_____

_____

_____

_____

_____

_____

_____

Part 2

Create a PowerPoint slide for each dressing/dip comparing the differences recorded in the chart. Present your findings to the class.

Activity 4.8
Lab—Advanced Garnishes

Directions

A garnish provides a special touch to a meal. In this lab you'll learn some simple and interesting garnishes that can be used for desserts, soups, and salads.

Recipe Selection

- Scallion Brush
- Pickle Fan
- Cucumber Fan
- Frosted Grapes

Objectives

After completing this lab activity, you should be able to:

- Apply effective *mise en place* through practice
- Demonstrate proper use of equipment and tools
- Follow basic food safety and sanitation guidelines
- Follow basic safety guidelines to avoid causing injury to self or others
- Prepare and serve a variety of garnishes

Directions

1. Review the recipe you have been assigned.
2. Perform *mise en place*.
3. Plan for any substitutions or additional ingredients you have been given.
4. Prepare the recipe.
5. Clean the area.

Scallion Brush

1. Gather supplies.

2. Cut off the root ends of the scallions (green onions), including the hard core.

3. Cut the white portion into 2″ sections.

4. Using the paring knife, split both ends of the scallion pieces with ½″-deep cuts.

5. Make enough cuts to separate the green portion into fine shreds.

6. Soak in ice water until the ends curl.

Pickle Fans

1. Gather supplies.

2. Hold the wide end (stem) of the pickle facing you.

3. Make a series of vertical cuts through the length of the pickle, but do not cut through the stem.

4. Gently separate the pickle into a fan. Be careful not to tear the pieces.

Cucumber Fan

1. Gather supplies.

2. Select firm, blemish-free cucumber.

3. Wash and dry the cucumber.

4. Use a channel knife to score the cucumber vertically from end to end. Space cuts evenly around the cucumber.

5. Begin slicing ⅛″- to ¼″- thick slices, being careful not to cut all the way through the cucumber. Leave approximately ¼″ of the flesh connected to the side of the cucumber to hold the rounds together.

6. Slice off the length of the fan that you want. Place this piece on the plate, and gently spread the fan open.

Frosted Grapes

1. Gather supplies.

2. Select small bunches of firm, unblemished grapes.

3. If necessary, separate into small bunches (5–10 grapes).

4. Brush the grapes with water.

5. Sprinkle with granulated sugar. If using dark grapes, you will want to use white sugar; for green grapes, you may choose to color the sugar a dark green for contrast.

6. Let the grapes dry before serving.

Activity 4.9
Lab—Chocolate Dessert Garnishes

Directions

You will be working with chocolate to create several different garnishes that can be used to complement a variety of desserts.

Grated Chocolate

This very simple garnish can be used to decorate a plate, or to add a splash of color to cake frosting or a simple pudding.

1. Gather a small bowl, a block of semisweet chocolate, and a grater.

2. Place the grater over the bowl and rub the chocolate over the grater to create a powder.

3. Store covered until needed.

Chocolate Shavings

1. Gather a paring knife, semisweet chocolate, and a small bowl.

2. Using the long end of the chocolate, take the paring knife, and pull it toward you to create chocolate curls. A vegetable peeler or parisienne scoop can also be used to create curls.

Chocolate Shards

1. Melt white chocolate or white chocolate bark in the microwave or on a double burner.

2. While chocolate is melting, line a baking sheet with waxed paper.

3. Fill a pastry bag, equipped with a small tip, with the melted white chocolate.

4. Pipe white chocolate on the waxed paper, making a loopy line that does not stop.

5. Let harden.

6. While the white chocolate loops are hardening, melt semisweet chocolate in a microwave or double burner.

7. Spread the dark chocolate over the piped white chocolate, creating a layer approximately ⅛″–¼″ thick.

8. Cool in a dry place.

9. When the chocolate has cooled, gently pull the waxed paper away.

10. Break the chocolate into irregularly shaped pieces. Cover and store in the refrigerator until ready to use.

11. Use to garnish cake slices, chocolate pies, mousses, etc.

Chocolate Strings

1. Melt chocolate in the microwave or double burner.

2. Fill a pastry bag, with a small tip, with the melted chocolate.

3. Pipe the chocolate in small designs on a waxed paper-lined baking sheet.

4. Allow to harden in a cool, dry place.

5. Gently remove waxed paper. Store in a covered container in the refrigerator until ready to use.

6. Can be used to garnish a variety of desserts.

Note:

On the back of the waxed paper, draw lines so you have a guide when creating the garnish. Turn the waxed paper over when ready to pipe the design.

Activity 4.10
Research—Edible Flowers

Directions

You have been asked by the local public television station to give a two- to three-minute presentation on edible flowers. For the presentation, they would like you to create a graphic (PowerPoint, chart, poster) that lists at least five different edible flowers, a picture of the flower, and a brief description of the characteristics of the flower.

In addition to the visual, be prepared to speak about the following points:

- History of edible flowers
- Where to purchase edible flowers
- How to choose safe flowers
- Garnishing cheese plates or desserts with edible flowers

Use the space provided below to take your notes. Use a separate sheet of paper, poster board, or your computer to create your final presentation.

Name of Flower	Description of Flower

Chapter **5**

Activity 5.1
Test Your Knowledge of Purchasing and Inventory IQ

Directions

Mark each of the following statements related to purchasing and inventory as either as either true (T) or false (F). For each false statement, rewrite it to make it a true statement.

Part 1—Introduction to Purchasing

_____ 1. The five major steps of the purchasing process include: determine the needs of the operation, identify quality standards, order products/services, receive deliveries, and store/issue products.

_____

_____

_____ 2. The first goal of purchasing is to make sure that the chef's favorite items are readily available.

_____

_____

_____ 3. Specifications are set by the manager to clearly communicate the quality standards for each item used by the operation.

_____

_____

_____ 4. Retailers are those who sell products directly to the public; therefore, a restaurant primarily would be considered a retailer.

_____

_____

_____ 5. Bids are rarely used by large operations when pricing products because a verbal price quote is all that is needed.

_____

_____

_____ 6. Kickbacks are money or goods received by a person in exchange for agreeing to buy products from a specific vendor.

_____

_____

Part 2—Making Purchasing Decisions

_____ 1. It is important for an operation to establish quality standards so that the customers receive a consistent product and experience.

_____

_____

_____ 2. A product specification is provided by the supplier to explain the products, features and benefits.

_____

_____

_____ 3. A make-or-buy analysis is conducted by an operation to determine whether it is more cost effective to make the item in-house or to buy it from a supplier.

_____

_____

_____ 4. A production sheet is used by the manager to schedule the appropriate number of kitchen staff for the day.

_____

_____

_____ 5. The sales mix report is used to track items that sell well and those that don't.

_____

_____

_____ 6. A purchase order is a legally binding written document that details what the buyer is purchasing from the supplier.

_____

_____

_____ 7. The two economic factors that influence the price of an item are supply and demand.

_____

_____

Part 3—Managing Purchases

_____ 1. The most important part of the receiving process is inspecting and rejecting deliveries.

_____

_____

_____ 2. An invoice is the supplier's bill listing the actual goods delivered to the buyer.

_____

_____

_____ 3. Perishable items should be stored in the cooler or freezer immediately after the delivery has been accepted.

_____

_____

_____ 4. When storing perishable items in the cooler, it is acceptable to place raw meats above ready-to-eat foods.

_____

_____

_____ 5. Issuing is the process of tracking food that leaves the storeroom through when it is put into production.

_____

_____

_____ 6. Inventory shrinkage applies to items such as steaks, which lose size during the cooking process.

_____

_____

Activity 5.2
Crossword Puzzle—Purchasing

Directions

Complete the following statements, and then use the answers to complete the crossword puzzle.

ACROSS

4. _____ _____ is the area designed to hold dry and canned foods.

8. A _____ _____ _____ analysis is used by an operation to determine whether it is more cost effective to make an item in-house or to purchase the item ready made from a vendor.

9. A _____ _____ _____ includes the particular businesses that buy and sell a product as it goes from the original source to the retailer.

11. The act of inspecting, accepting, and possibly rejecting deliveries is known as _____.

12. The ideal amount of inventory items that an operation should have on hand at all times in order to avoid stockouts is known as _____ _____.

14. Items on the menu that don't sell well are also called _____.

15. _____ occur when the restaurant runs out of a menu item.

DOWN

1. _____ is short for furniture, fixtures, and equipment.

2. The _____ _____ of items sold identifies menu items that have been most popular.

3. A _____ is notice of a price that a supplier gives to the buyer during the purchasing process.

5. _____ are set by the manager, chef, or owner and are used to clearly communicate quality standards to vendors.

6. There are two types of _____ methods used in restaurants, physical and perpetual.

7. The amount of water moisture in the air is called _____.

9. A _____ _____ is issued by the delivery person when an item is rejected during delivery.

10. _____ are food items that have a constant demand, for example, flour.

13. _____ are specialized, written price lists created for the restaurant by the supplier.

www.CrosswordWeaver.com

Activity 5.3
Career Exploration—The Buyer

Directions

The buyer has a unique job position that requires a wide variety of skills. Using your textbook, the career center, and online resources, research the position of buyer within the restaurant and foodservice industry. Write a one- to two-page report that discusses the job of a buyer, the educational requirements, unique demands of the job, salary, and opportunities for growth and advancement. Complete the paper with a list of hospitality companies that might have a buyer, and explain why you may or may not find this position interesting.

Take your notes below. Use additional sheets of paper or your computer to create your final paper.

_____

_____

_____

_____

_____

_____

_____

_____

_____

_____

_____

_____

_____

_____

_____

_____

_____

_____

_____

_____

_____

_____

Activity 5.4
Product Specifications

Directions

You have been hired as the chef for a new restaurant that will be opening in six weeks. The owner has asked you to create the product specifications for the following items that will be used on the new menu. Using the space provided or word processing software, complete the product specifications.

Easy Street Café New Menu Items

- ¼-lb Burger served with choice of American cheese, cheddar cheese, or bacon; Garnished with a slice of lettuce, pickle spear, tomato, and onion.
- Bacon, lettuce, and tomato sandwich served on white toast
- Include the following items in your product specification:
  - Intended use
  - Brand name (if applicable)
  - Exact name
  - Market form
  - Packaging
  - Size
  - USDA grade (if applicable)

Product Specification Sheet

	Description
Intended use	
Brand name	
Exact name	
Market form	
Packaging	
Size	
USDA grade	

Product Specification Sheet

	Description
Intended use	
Brand name	
Exact name	
Market form	
Packaging	
Size	
USDA grade	

Activity 5.5
Lab—Make-or-Buy Analysis

Directions

You have been asked to conduct a make-or-buy analysis for the Easy Street Café. The manager of the café is considering adding jumbo oatmeal raisin cookies to the menu. She expects to sell at least four dozen cookies per day and needs a recommendation on whether it will be more cost effective to make or buy the cookies.

Using the recipe provided, make a batch of jumbo oatmeal raisin cookies. Use the worksheet below to record your cost of ingredients and also to record the amount of time spent preparing and baking the cookies. After baking the cookies, contact the local bakery or bakeshop within a grocery store and find out the price for a similar cookie. You may also want to check an online grocery store such as http://peapod.com. After gathering your data, write a short one- to two-paragraph recommendation to the manager explaining your recommendation to either make or buy the cookies.

Oatmeal Raisin Cookies

Yield: 8 dozen (approximately)   Serving Size: 1 cookie

Measure	Ingredients
2¼ lb	All-purpose flour
1 oz	Baking soda
½ oz	Cinnamon, ground
½ oz	Salt
3 lb	Butter, soft
1 lb, 3 oz	Sugar
3½ lb	Light brown sugar
10	Eggs
1 fl oz	Vanilla extract
3 lb, 3 oz	Rolled oats
1½ lb	Raisins

Directions

1. Line sheet pans with parchment paper.

2. Sift together the flour, baking soda, cinnamon, and salt.

3. Cream the butter and sugars on medium speed with a paddle attachment until the mixture is smooth and light in color, about 10 minutes. Scrape down the bowl periodically.

4. Blend the eggs and vanilla.

5. Add the egg-vanilla mixture to the butter-sugar mixture in three additions. Mix until fully incorporated. After each addition, scrape down the bowl as needed.

6. On low speed, mix in the sifted dry ingredients and the oats and raisins until just incorporated.

7. Scale the dough into 3-oz portions.

8. Arrange on the prepared sheet pans in even rows.

9. Bake at 375°F until the cookies are lightly brown, about 12 minutes.

10. Allow to cool slightly on the pans.

11. Transfer to racks to cool completely.

Cost Analysis Sheet
Oatmeal Cookie Prepared On Site

Description	Quantity	Unit Cost	Extension
Flour	2¼ lb		
Baking soda	1 oz		
Ground cinnamon	½ oz		
Salt	½ oz		
Butter	3 lb		
Sugar	1 lb, 3 oz		
Eggs	10		
Vanilla extract	1 fl oz		
Rolled oats	3 lb, 3 oz		
Raisins	1½ lb		
	Subtotal		
	Cost per cookie		

Parchment paper cost: _____

Labor

Number of hours involved in preparation: _____

Hourly wage: _____

Labor cost: _____

(Labor cost = Hours × Wage)

Cost Analysis Sheet
Oatmeal Cookie Purchased from Vendor

Yield:

Serving Size:

Description	Quantity	Unit Cost	Extension
Oatmeal raisin cookie			
	Sub-total		
	Delivery charge		
	Total		

Take your notes in the space below. Present your findings to the class.

_____

_____

_____

_____

_____

_____

_____

_____

_____

_____

_____

_____

_____

_____

_____

_____

_____

_____

_____

_____

_____

Activity 5.6
Practice Purchase Order

Directions

Calculate the correct dollar amounts and totals for the following purchase order.

Purchase Order

Item	Description	Quantity	Unit Cost	Extension
1.	Canned peas	6 cases	$11.75/case	
2.	California carrots, U.S. Extra Fancy, No. 1	6 cases	$ 7.87/case	
3.	Cod fillets, boneless, no skin	40 lb	$2.35/lb	
4.	Cheddar cheese, Wisconsin aged	2 cases	$1.35/lb (8 lb/case)	
5.	Tomato juice	3 cases	$8.98/case	
6.	Olives, ripe	4 qt	$12.55/qt	
7.	Fresh cabbage	5 cases	$13.75/case	
8.	Washington apples, fresh Rome Beauty	2 cases	$19.65/case	
9.	Red tomatoes, U.S. No. 1	2 cases	$5.85/case	
10.	Hamburger, IMPS No. 136	150 lb	$1.64/lb	
11.	Eggs, fresh, in shell, U.S. AA	2 cases	$0.98/doz 15 doz/case	
12.	Garlic powder	2 cans	$0.76/can	
13.	Kosher dill pickles	2 gal	$9.67/gal	
14.	Fresh-frozen crab meat	45 lb	$27.50/lb	
15.	Green onions	20 bunches	$0.34/bunch	
16.	Shrimp, headless, frozen, in shell (21–30)	18 packages	$25.00/lb (5 lb/package)	
			Sub-total	
			Tax (9.25% for subtotal)	
			Delivery	$75.00
			Total	

Activity 5.7
Put Your Order in Order

Directions

Part 1

Answer the following questions based on what you have learned about receiving, storing, and issuing in Chapter 5.

1. When receiving a delivery, you notice the invoice lists ten cases of tomatoes. The actual delivery only includes nine cases of tomatoes. Can you think of a way to handle the situation at the moment, and what could you use to substitute for the tomatoes if it is needed?

_____

_____

_____

_____

_____

2. What are the two most common methods used to track foodservice inventories? What are the similarities and differences between these two methods? Which would you prefer to use in your restaurant? Why?

_____

_____

_____

_____

_____

3. Describe the difference between issuing and pilfering.

_____

_____

_____

_____

_____

Part 2

Number the steps of the purchasing process in the order in which they are performed, with 1 being the first step and 9 being the last step.

Order   Item

_____   A. Fill out a receiving sheet.

_____   B. Prepare and submit purchase orders.

_____   C. Properly store items, using the FIFO principle to rotate stock.

_____   D. Review invoice that accompanies the delivery.

_____   E. Select supplier who gives you the best mix (price, product, quality, and supplier services).

_____   F. Review or plan all menus.

_____   G. Have employees issue food from storage into the kitchen area as needed.

_____   H. Request written price bids or verbal quotes from suppliers.

_____   I. Write specifications list.

Activity 5.8
Poster—Preventing Spoilage and Cross-Contamination

Directions

You have been asked by your manager to create a training poster that can be used with new hires and also as a refresher for existing employees to encourage safe practices for storing raw and cooked food. Be creative, but also emphasize the importance of safe food storage practices in order to prevent a foodborne-illness outbreak in the operation. Include information on storing the following items:

- Leftovers
- Seafood
- Beef or pork (raw and cooked)
- Ground meat
- Poultry
- Vegetables
- Eggs
- Beverages

The poster can be created using poster board, the space provided below, or your computer. The poster should include images of the different food items, suggestions for storing, and ways to maximize space safely within the refrigerator.

Activity 5.9
Calculating the Cost of Purchasing

Directions

Complete the food cost worksheet and then calculate the food cost percentage and possible losses to the restaurant.

Part 1

At the close of business on September 30, Maria and Alfred were asked to help with month-end inventory. Each employee was provided with a list of products that had been purchased by the restaurant during the month of September. Maria and Alfred were responsible for counting all the items on the shelves in dry storage and in the coolers and freezers so the manager could complete the inventory. At the end of the night, the numbers looked like this:

Date	Action	Amount
9/1	Opening inventory:	$45,271
9/7	Delivery (cost of goods received)	+$5,567
9/14	Delivery (cost of goods received)	+$12,059
9/21	Delivery (cost of goods received)	+$_____
9/28	Delivery (cost of goods received)	+$4,523
	Total	$77,876
10/1	Ending inventory	$32,678
(9/1-9/30)	Total cost of food	$_____

Complete the chart by filling in the missing goods received and calculating the total and also the total cost of food.

Part 2

Using the information below and the numbers provided in the chart, answer the following questions:

1. The manager was pleased to see the food inventory value was consistent with similar month's sales and invoices. Sales during September had been a little lower than expected; however, the chef had ordered the same amount of product as if the forecast was met. If sales for the restaurant were $150,000, what was the food cost percentage?

_____

_____

_____

_____

_____

2. The original sales forecast was $175,000 in food sales. If the inventory levels remained the same but the sales forecast was met, what would the food cost percentage have been?

_____

_____

_____

_____

_____

3. Based on the monthly restaurant sales and the total cost of food for September, did the restaurant have a profit or loss for the month?

_____

_____

_____

_____

_____

Activity 5.10
Receiving Guidelines

Directions

You have been asked by the manager of the Easy Street Café to create a portion of the training manual that will be used by new employees. The manager selected you because you have completed coursework in culinary arts and foodservice management, and he feels confident that you are the best person for the job. This task requires two elements. The first is a one- to two-page list of best practices for receiving. The second is a checklist that should be used by anyone receiving a delivery.

In your list of best practices, be sure to include information on the following:

- How to prepare for the delivery
- What to look for when the delivery arrives
  - Seafood
  - Meat
  - Poultry
  - Dairy and eggs
  - Frozen products
  - Dry goods
- What to look for when comparing the invoice to the actual goods received
- Recording the delivery
- Requesting a credit
- Where to store products

The checklist should include an abbreviated version of the manual and visuals. The checklist is to be posted at the loading dock.

Use a separate sheet of paper or your computer to create your final training material.

Chapter **6**

Activity 6.1
Test Your Meat, Poultry, and Seafood IQ

Directions

Mark each of the following statements related to meat, poultry, and seafood as either true (T) or false (F). For each false statement, rewrite it to make it a true statement.

Part 1—Meat

_____ 1. A USDA stamp on meat means that it is wholesome and safe to eat.

_____

_____

_____ 2. There are several USDA grades for meat, and those labeled Choice are the best possible grade.

_____

_____

_____ 3. Fabrication is the process used to butcher primal cuts of meat into usable portions.

_____

_____

_____ 4. Offal meat is used to make medallions or scallops and is tender and juicy.

_____

_____

_____ 5. Marbling in meat refers to the lines of fat within the lean flesh portion of the meat.

_____

_____

_____ 6. When receiving meat deliveries, meat that is brown or green in color can be accepted provided it will be used within 24 hours.

_____

_____

_____ 7. Dry heat cooking is a common method used for naturally tender cuts of meat.

_____

_____

_____ 8. Barding is a technique used to add a layer of fat to meats that have little or no natural fat.

_____

_____

Part 2—Poultry

_____ 1. The USDA is responsible for grading poultry, and grades of A, B, C, or D are given based on the size of the bird.

_____

_____

_____ 2. There are two types of meat found in poultry, white and dark, and each has a different taste and nutritional value.

_____

_____

_____ 3. When boning poultry, the butcher is separating the meat from the bones and cutting the bird into pieces.

_____

_____

_____ 4. Poultry that has purple or green around the neck signifies a high-quality bird.

_____

_____

_____ 5. When roasting a bird, it is important to truss it so that the bird cooks evenly and stays moist.

_____

_____

_____ 6. Poultry should be cooked to an internal temperature of 140°F to kill all traces of *Salmonella* spp.

_____

_____

Part 3—Seafood

_____ 1. Seafood that has been inspected by the U.S. Department of Commerce (USDC) carries the PUFI (Processed Under Federal Inspection) mark.

_____

_____

_____ 2. There are four main categories of fish: fin fish, flatfish, roundfish, and shellfish.

_____

_____

_____ 3. Most shellfish served in restaurants are crustaceans, particularly lobsters, craps, shrimp, and crayfish.

_____

_____

_____ 4. Fresh fish are very sensitive to time-temperature abuse and must be handled correctly to avoid spoiling.

_____

_____

_____ 5. Shellfish must have shellstock identification tags, which must be retained for at least 30 days after the item was delivered.

_____

_____

_____ 6. The best way to cook fin fish is with dry heat and high temperatures.

_____

_____

Part 4—Charcuterie and Garde Manger

_____ 1. Charcuterie is a German term meaning "spicy meat."

_____

_____

_____ 2. The garde manger chef is responsible for the preparation of cold foods, including salads and cold appetizers.

_____

_____

_____ 3. Forcemeat is the primary ingredient found in paté.

_____

_____

_____ 4. A forcemeat made of exotic game, such as mouse, is called a mousseline.

_____

_____

Activity 6.2
Editorial—The Importance of Meat for Good Nutrition

Directions

Write an editorial about the importance of beef (or other meat) in the daily diet. Or, if you feel that meat is not key to a healthy diet—that individuals can get all necessary nutrients without eating meat—write your editorial from that standpoint. Find statistics on the Internet about the importance of meats in maintaining good health. Use the material in *Chapter 6: Meat, Poultry, and Seafood* as a starting point.

Take your notes in the space below. Attach additional pages as necessary.

_____

_____

_____

_____

_____

_____

_____

_____

_____

_____

_____

_____

_____

_____

_____

_____

_____

_____

_____

Activity 6.3
Lab—Cooking with Beef

Directions

Meat refers to beef, veal, lamb, mutton, or pork, and most diners expect to see a variety of meat dishes on the menu. In this lab, you will have the opportunity to prepare dishes using a variety of cuts of beef.

Recipe Selection

- Beef Stroganoff
- Chicken Fried Steak
- London Broil
- Meatloaf
- Swiss Steak

Objectives

After completing this lab activity, you should be able to:

- Apply effective *mise en place* through practice
- Demonstrate proper use of equipment and tools
- Follow basic food safety and sanitation guidelines
- Follow basic safety guidelines to avoid causing injury to self or others
- Prepare and serve a variety of meats

Directions

1. Review the recipe you have been assigned.
2. Perform *mise en place*.
3. Plan for any substitutions or additional ingredients you have been given.
4. Prepare the recipe.
5. Clean the area.

Beef Stroganoff

Yield: 6 servings

Measure	Ingredients
2 tbsp	All-purpose flour
1 tsp	Salt
¼ tsp	Pepper
3 lb	Beef tenderloin, trimmed and cut into large dice
4 tbsp	Butter, oil, or other fat
3 c	Mushrooms, ¼″ slices
1 c	Onions, julienne
2 cloves	Garlic, roasted, minced
½ qt	Brown stock
2 tbsp	Tomato paste
2 c	Sour cream

Directions

1. Combine flour with salt and pepper. Dredge beef in flour mixture.

2. Heat butter or oil in a saucepan. Add beef and brown quickly on both sides.

3. Add mushrooms, onions, and garlic and sauté for 5–7 minutes.

4. Add a little of the stock to deglaze the pan. Add the remaining stock and tomato paste, and reduce for 3–5 minutes.

5. Slowly add the sour cream, and bring to a gentle simmer. Return meat, and slowly simmer for 5 minutes, making sure not to boil and that meat is tender.

Suggestion

Serve over egg noodles, and garnish with sliced mushrooms, deep-fried chives, and shallots.

© **Michael Zema, FMP/CCE. Used with permission.**

Chicken Fried Steak

Yield: 8 servings

Measure	Ingredients
3 lb	Beef round steak, ½″ thick
2	Eggs
¼ c	Milk
½ tsp	Salt
¼ tsp	Pepper
2 c	Panko breadcrumbs (or other coarse breadcrumb)
1 c	Vegetable or olive oil

Directions

1. Tenderize the steak by pounding to half its thickness.
2. Combine eggs, milk, salt, and pepper. Mix well. (This is the egg wash.)
3. Dip steaks in the egg mixture, and then coat with breadcrumbs.
4. Discard any unused egg mixture or breadcrumbs.
5. Add steaks, and sauté on both sides until golden brown, turning only once.
6. Cover steaks, and place in a 300°F oven for 45–60 minutes. Cooking times will vary depending on oven.

Suggestions

Use ½ milk and ½ veal stock in place of milk to make egg wash.

Serve with mashed potatoes and brown gravy, cooked carrots, and garnish with chopped parsley.

© Michael Zema, FMP/CCE. Used with permission.

London Broil

Yield: 6 servings

Measure	Ingredients
1 c	Oil
¼ c	Wine, balsamic, cider, or other flavored vinegar
½ tsp	Salt
¼ tsp	Pepper
1 pinch	Italian-blend seasoning
2 cloves	Garlic, minced
3 lb	Beef flank steak, trimmed and scored on both sides

Directions

1. In a large bowl, whisk all ingredients together, except the beef.

2. Add beef, cover, and marinate 3–4 hours.

3. Remove beef from marinade, draining excess marinade.

4. Place beef on preheated grill or broiler. Grill or broil 5–7 minutes on each side, turning only once, and lightly season with salt and pepper when cooking. For best results, cook rare to medium rare.

5. Remove from heat, and slice very thinly across the grain.

© Michael Zema, FMP/CCE. Used with permission.

Meatloaf

Yield: 8 servings

Measure	Ingredients
2	Eggs
1½ c	Milk
1 c	Panko breadcrumbs (or other coarse breadcrumb)
3 oz	Onion, small dice
1 tbsp	Italian parsley, snipped
1 tsp	Fresh oregano, minced
1 tsp	Fresh thyme, minced
2 tsp	Kosher salt
1 tsp	Ground sage
¼ tsp	Pepper
3 lb	Ground beef
½ c	Ketchup
3 tbsp	Brown sugar
2 tsp	Dijon mustard

Directions

1. Preheat oven to 350°F.

2. In a large bowl, combine eggs and milk. Mix well.

3. Add breadcrumbs, onions, parsley, oregano, thyme, salt, pepper, and ground beef. Mix very well.

4. Place meatloaf in a lightly greased 8″ × 4″ × 2″ loaf pan. Place in preheated oven and bake for 60–70 minutes.

5. Mix ketchup, sugar, and mustard to make a sauce. Ladle over meatloaf, and return to oven for an additional 10 minutes.

Suggestion

Serve with garlic mashed potatoes.

© **Michael Zema, FMP/CCE. Used with permission.**

Swiss Steak

Yield: 8 servings

Measure	Ingredients
4 tbsp	All-purpose flour
As needed	Salt
As needed	Pepper
4 lb	Beef round steak, cut into ¾″ slices
As needed	Oil
1 oz	Onions, bâtonnet
6 oz	Carrots, small dice
8 oz	Celery, small dice
2 cloves	Garlic, minced
1 (16 oz) can	Diced, stewed, or fire-roasted tomatoes, undrained
½ qt	Beef stock
1	Sachet

Directions

1. Combine flour with salt and pepper. Dredge steaks in flour mixture. Discard any unused flour mixture.

2. Heat oil in a brazier. Add beef, and brown on all sides. Add onions, carrots, celery, and garlic and sauté for 5–7 minutes.

3. Add tomatoes; use liquids from the tomatoes to deglaze pan.

4. Add beef and sachet. Cover and simmer for 60–75 minutes, or until tender. Occasionally skim off impurities and excess fat.

5. Remove beef and reserve in a warm place. Check sauce for consistency. If too thick, add additional stock to thin out. If too thin, reduce until desired consistency. Strain sauce, and return to brazier.

6. Adjust flavor with salt and pepper.

7. If meat is not tender, pour sauce over meat, add a little more stock, and simmer until desired doneness.

8. At service time, ladle sauce over meat and serve.

© **Michael Zema, FMP/CCE. Used with permission.**

Activity 6.4
Match the Cut to the Best Cooking Technique

Directions

Meat is one of the most-expensive products on the menu. Knowing the best methods for preparing meat so that there is little waste and high-guest satisfaction is essential for a successful restaurant. In this exercise, match the type of meat with the best cooking method.

Cooking methods will be used multiple times.

Beef	
	Rib Roast
	Tenderloin
	Flank Steak
	Brisket
Veal	
	Rib
	Veal Shank
	Veal Loin Chop
	Kidney
Pork	
	Boston Butt
	Ham
	Bacon
	Spareribs

1	Grill
2	Roasting
3	Moist heat
4	Combination
5	Dry heat

Activity 6.5
Lab—How to Cut Chicken Eight Ways

Directions

Knowing how to fabricate (break down) a chicken into eight parts is an essential skill that is needed by workers in a professional kitchen. In this lab, you will break down a chicken, and identify the parts of the bird.

Objectives

After completing this lab activity, you should be able to:

- Apply effective *mise en place* through practice
- Demonstrate proper use of equipment and tools
- Follow basic food safety and sanitation guidelines
- Follow basic safety guidelines to avoid causing injury to self or others
- Demonstrate how to breakdown a chicken into eight parts
- Identify the primary parts of the chicken

Directions

1. Perform *mise en place.*
2. Plan for any substitutions or additional ingredients you have been given.
3. Prepare the chicken.
4. Clean the area.

Directions

1. Square up the bird by placing it on its back and pressing on the legs and breast to create a uniform appearance.

2. Remove the leg and thigh from the body by cutting between the joints close to the bones in the back of the bird. Repeat for the other side.

3. Place the bird on its breast and cut through the skin and straight down either side of the backbone from tail to head.

4. Cut the ribs that connect the backbone, removing the backbone.

5. Cut the breast into 2 pieces by placing the chicken skin side down; start cutting at the wishbone, separating the breast into 2 halves. Bending the sides of the bird backwards beforehand will make it easier to cut.

6. Separate the leg from the thigh by making a cut following the line of fat on the inside of the thigh. Do this with the skin side down and cut through the joint.

7. Separate the wings from the breast by pulling the wing away from the body, and then cut inside each wing along the joint. You should now have 2 wings, 2 breasts, 2 legs, and 2 thighs.

Note:

Refer to Page 383 in the text for pictures to support this process.

Activity 6.6
Lab—Cooking with Poultry

Directions

Poultry is a versatile product that can be used in many ways in the kitchen. The bones can be used to create a tasty soup or broth, while the meat can be served in a salad, as a main course, or as a tasty appetizer such as chicken wings. In this lab, we'll focus on chicken, as a mainstay in many restaurants.

Recipe Selection

- Chicken Cacciatore
- Chicken and Dumplings
- Roast Chicken with Rosemary
- Chicken Stir-fry

Objectives

After completing this lab activity, you should be able to:

- Apply effective *mise en place* through practice
- Demonstrate proper use of equipment and tools
- Follow basic food safety and sanitation guidelines
- Follow basic safety guidelines to avoid causing injury to self or others
- Prepare and serve a variety of poultry dishes

Directions

1. Review the recipe you have been assigned.
2. Perform *mise en place*.
3. Plan for any substitutions or additional ingredients you have been given.
4. Prepare the recipe.
5. Clean the area.

Chicken Cacciatore

Yield: 8 servings

Measure	Ingredients
4 tbsp	Olive oil
8	Chicken breasts, boneless, skin on
2 oz	Shallots, brunoise
2 cloves	Roasted garlic, minced
1 c	Mushrooms, assorted, sliced
1 tsp	Italian blend seasoning
½ c	Chicken stock and tomato liquid (equal parts)
2 (16 oz) cans	Tomatoes, diced, stewed, or fire-roasted
2 tbsp	Flour
To taste	Salt
To taste	Pepper

Directions

1. Heat olive oil in a large sauté pan. Dust the chicken breast lightly with flour and brown on all sides. Remove and reserve.

2. Add shallots and garlic to pan and sweat for 3-5 minutes. Add mushrooms and Italian seasoning and continue sautéing for 3 minutes.

3. Deglaze pan with half of the tomato liquid-stock mixture.

4. Drain liquid from tomato product, and reserve. Add tomatoes to pan, and simmer for 3-5 minutes.

5. Return chicken to pan, and simmer.

6. Mix flour with remaining tomato-stock mixture and additional reserved tomato liquid to make a slurry.

7. Add slurry to pan, mix well, cover, and simmer for 15-20 minutes, making sure slurry is cooked.

8. Adjust sauce with salt and pepper.

© **Michael Zema, FMP/CCE. Used with permission.**

Chicken and Dumplings

Yield: 6 servings

Base

Measure	Ingredients
1 (4 lb)	Chicken, whole
3 qt	Water
3 c	Onion, chopped
1 c	Celery, chopped
1 c	Carrot, chopped
1 tsp	Salt
¼ tsp	Pepper
10	Garlic cloves, peeled
4	Thyme sprigs
2	Bay leaves
¼ c	All-purpose flour
2 tsp	Cornstarch
3 tbsp	Heavy cream

Directions

1. Remove neck and giblets from chicken, and discard.

2. Rinse chicken, and pat dry.

3. Place in 8-quart stockpot, and add water, onion, celery, carrots, salt, pepper, garlic, thyme, and bay leaves.

4. Bring to a boil, and then turn down heat and simmer 45 minutes (or until vegetables are tender). Skim the surface occasionally to remove any solids.

5. Remove from heat.

6. Remove chicken from the pot; cool. Strain stock through a china cap into a large bowl. Reserve carrots and celery, if you like.

7. Remove the chicken meat from the bones, and tear the pieces into bite-sized bits (approximately 2"). Store in refrigerator until needed.

8. Cool stock in refrigerator. When stock has cooled, removed the layer of fat that has formed on the top, and discard.

9. Reheat stock over medium high heat until it boils, and then reduce heat and simmer until reduced to eight cups broth.

10. Heat a cast iron skillet for 5 minutes over medium-high heat. Add ¼ cup flour to the pan, and cook for 1 minute or until lightly browned; stir constantly.

11. Combine browned flour with the cornstarch in a large bowl. Add ⅔ cup of the stock to the flour mixture, and whisk until smooth.

12. Add the flour mixture to the remaining stock, and bring to a boil. Cook for 2 minutes or until slightly thickened.

13. Reduce heat, and stir in heavy cream. Add the chicken, and simmer over low heat.

Dumplings

Measure	Ingredients
¾ c	Milk
1	Egg, large
1½ c	All-purpose flour
1 tbsp	Baking powder
1 tbsp	Cornmeal
½ tsp	Salt
1 tbsp	Parsley, chopped

Directions

1. In a medium bowl, combine the milk and eggs.

2. Combine the flour, baking powder, and salt in a small bowl.

3. Add the flour mixture to the milk mixture.

4. Stir with a fork until dry ingredients are moist.

5. Drop ⅓ of the dumpling batter by teaspoonful into the chicken mixture. Cover, and cook for 3 minutes or until dumplings are done. (Do not boil the mixture.)

6. Remove dumplings with a slotted spoon, and place in a serving bowl, keeping them warm.

7. Repeat steps 5 and 6 until all the dumpling dough has been used.

8. Remove the chicken mixture from the heat, and pour over the dumplings.

9. Garnish with chopped parsley.

Roast Chicken with Rosemary

Yield: 6 servings

Measure	Ingredients
1 (3 lb)	Chicken, whole roaster
To taste	Salt
To taste	Pepper
1–2 tsp	Olive oil
1	Onion, small, quartered
¼ c	Rosemary, fresh chopped

Directions

1. Preheat oven to 350°F.

2. Rinse the chicken thoroughly and blot dry.

3. Season the inside and outside of the chicken generously with salt and pepper, and rub with olive oil.

4. Place the onion and rosemary inside the cavity of the chicken. Truss the chicken.

5. Place the chicken on a rack in a roasting pan.

6. Roast for 2–2½ hours or until an instant read thermometer inserted at the thickest point of the thigh reads 165°F.

Chicken Stir-fry

Yield: 4 servings

Measure	Ingredients
1 lb	Chicken breasts, boneless, skinless
3 tbsp	Cornstarch
2 tbsp	Soy sauce, reduced sodium
½ tsp	Ginger, ground
¼ tsp	Garlic powder
3 tbsp	Vegetable oil
2 c	Broccoli florets
1 c	Celery, sliced
1 c	Carrots, thinly sliced
1	Onion, small, wedges
1 c	Reduced sodium chicken stock or broth

Directions

1. Cut chicken into ½″ strips.

2. Combine soy sauce, garlic powder, and corn starch and whisk together.

3. Toss sauce with the chicken to coat. Refrigerate, covered, for 30 minutes.

4. In a large skillet or wok, heat two tablespoons of oil.

5. Stir-fry the chicken until no longer pink, about 3–5 minutes. Remove the chicken from the pan, and place in a clean bowl.

6. Add the remaining oil to the pan, and stir-fry the broccoli, celery, carrots, and onions for 4–5 minutes, or until tender crisp.

7. Add chicken stock or broth.

8. Return chicken to pan, and cook until heated through and sauce becomes thick and bubbly.

9. Serve immediately.

Activity 6.7
Research—Sushi

Directions

A new sushi bar has opened in town. The manager of the store has asked that you create an ad to encourage more customers to try sushi. In order to do this successfully, you will need to research what sushi is, where the main ingredients for many popular types of sushi come from, and then create either a print ad or a 30-second radio ad to encourage people to eat more sushi.

Take your notes in the space below. Use a separate sheet of paper, poster board, or your computer to create your ad.

_____

_____

_____

_____

_____

_____

_____

_____

_____

_____

_____

_____

_____

_____

_____

_____

_____

_____

_____

_____

Activity 6.8
Lab—Cooking with Seafood

Directions

Seafood includes both fin fish and shellfish, and many restaurants will offer at least a few seafood options for guests who are looking for variety in the menu. Seafood is versatile, can be prepared in many ways, and requires a skilled hand to prepare it properly. In this lab, you will have the opportunity to see three different seafood preparation methods.

Recipe Selection

- Sautéed Trout Meuniere
- Broiled Lemon Sole on a Bed of Leeks
- Grilled Fish Steaks

Objectives

After completing this lab activity, you should be able to:

- Apply effective *mise en place* through practice
- Demonstrate proper use of equipment and tools
- Follow basic food safety and sanitation guidelines
- Follow basic safety guidelines to avoid causing injury to self or others
- Prepare and serve a variety of seafood

Directions

1. Review the recipe you have been assigned.
2. Perform *mise en place.*
3. Plan for any substitutions or additional ingredients you have been given.
4. Prepare the recipe.
5. Clean the area.

Sautéed Trout Meunière

Yield: 10 servings

Measure	Ingredients
10	Trout, pan-dressed, about 10 oz each
To taste	Salt
To taste	Pepper
As needed	All-purpose flour
2 oz	Oil (or butter)
2 oz	Lemon juice
3 tbsp	Parsley, chopped

Directions

1. Rinse the trout.

2. Trim the trout as necessary, removing the head and tail, if desired.

3. When ready to sauté, blot dry, and season with salt and pepper.

4. Dredge the fish in flour, shaking off any excess.

5. Heat a sauté pan to medium-high.

6. Add the oil or butter.

7. Sauté the trout until the flesh is opaque and firm, about 3 minutes per side.

8. Remove the trout from the pan. Keep the trout warm on heated plates while completing the sauce.

9. To begin preparing the sauce, pour off the excess fat from the pan.

10. Add whole butter (about 1 oz per portion).

11. Cook until the butter begins to brown and has a nutty aroma.

12. Add the lemon juice.

13. Swirl the pan to deglaze it.

14. Add the parsley, and immediately pour or spoon the pan sauce over the trout.

15. Serve immediately.

Baked Lemon Sole on a Bed of Leeks

Yield: 10 servings

Measure	Ingredients
3¾ lb	Sole fillet
1½ oz	Lemon juice
½ tsp	Salt
¼ tsp	Black pepper, freshly ground
1 oz	Butter
6 oz	Bread crumbs, white, fresh
2 oz	Butter, unsalted
1½ lb	Leeks, julienned
4 oz	Heavy cream

Directions

1. Preheat the broiler.
2. Cut the fish into 10 equal 6-ounce portions (or 2, 3-ounce pieces per portion).
3. Season the fish with the lemon juice and half of the salt and pepper.
4. Brush the fish with ½ ounce of butter (melted).
5. Work the remaining ½ ounce butter into the breadcrumbs to moisten them slightly.
6. Coat the top of the fish with the breadcrumbs.
7. Place the sizzle plate 4″ under the broiler.
8. Broil undisturbed for about 4 minutes, or until the fish is done and the topping is browned.
9. Melt the butter in a large sauté pan.
10. Add the leeks.
11. Cover.
12. Stew gently until the leeks are tender, about 6–8 minutes.
13. Season the leeks with the remaining salt and pepper.
14. Add the cream.
15. Reduce slightly, about two minutes.
16. Serve the fish on a bed of 4 ounces of stewed leeks.

Grilled Fish Steaks

Yield: 6 servings

Measure	Ingredients
3 oz	Lemon juice, or a combination of citrus flavors
3 oz	Clarified butter or oil
6 (6 oz)	Tuna, salmon, or swordfish steaks
As needed	Salt
As needed	Pepper
As needed	Paprika

Directions

1. Mix lemon juice with clarified butter or oil. Brush mixture on both sides of steaks, and lightly season with salt, pepper, and paprika.

2. Place steaks directly on medium-hot grill and grill, turning once and brushing with remaining butter to prevent dryness.

3. Continue grilling until steaks are gently firm, about 10 minutes.

© **Michael Zema, FMP/CCE. Used with permission.**

Activity 6.9
Presentation—Sustainable Seafood

Directions

You have been asked by a group of local chefs to give a presentation about seafood. In particular, the group would like to learn more about the sustainability of a select group of fish. There are seven fish on the chefs' list, and the club has given you the flexibility to select just one of these fish for your presentation. The fish are:

- Chilean Sea Bass

- Orange Roughy

- Salmon (including farmed)

- Shark

- Shrimp (all types)

- Swordfish

- Bluefin Tuna

The group of chefs includes those who work extensively with seafood and those who occasionally offer seafood on their menus. They not only are interested in fishing methods, but also in learning more about how these fish can be protected. In your presentation, include the following information:

- The name of the fish you are discussing and a picture(s) of the fish

- The primary areas where the fish can be found—include a map

- What methods are used to catch these fish?

- Where is the largest market for this fish?

- Is the fish a sustainable resource?

- If the fish isn't considered sustainable at this time, how can people increase the fish population?

- What is the best method for cooking this fish?

- Share a recipe using this fish.

Use a separate sheet of paper, poster board, or your computer to create your presentation. Present your findings to the class.

Activity 6.10
Menu Design—Sausages around the World

Directions

You are working with the catering manager of a large banquet facility on a special request from a local group. They are celebrating their 50th anniversary as an organization and wanted to create a special buffet that honors their members around the globe. The challenge is to create a buffet menu for 100 people using several unique stations. Each station must feature a sausage from a different country and at least three complementary food items (starch, vegetables, etc.). According to the client, money is no object. Each station must be decorated to represent the country and include a description of each menu item.

Country List (choose one):

- France
- Germany
- Poland
- United States
- Greece
- Italy
- Canada
- United Kingdom
- Mexico
- South America
- China
- Philippines
- North Africa
- Australia

Using the space provided below, list your buffet items. Include the description of the items—be creative—and what you would use to decorate the tables. Use a separate sheet of paper, poster board, or your computer to create your final poster.

_____

_____

_____

_____

_____

_____

_____

_____

_____

_____

_____

_____

_____

_____

Chapter **7**

Activity 7.1
Test Your Knowledge of Marketing IQ

Directions

Mark each of the following statements related to marketing as either as either true (T) or false (F). For each false statement, rewrite it to make it a true statement.

Part 1—Introduction to Marketing

_____ 1. Marketing is the process of communicating a business's message to its audience.

_____

_____

_____ 2. Advertising and marketing are the same thing, as both are designed to increase business.

_____

_____

_____ 3. The marketing mix refers to the components that go into a successful print ad, i.e., the layout, message, and colors.

_____

_____

_____ 4. A marketing plan is the list of steps an operation must follow to sell a product or service to their target audience (market).

_____

_____

_____ 5. A SWOT analysis is conducted when an operation feels there is too much competition.

_____

_____

_____ 6. In a SWOT analysis, a "threat" refers to factors outside the operation that could cause a decrease in revenue.

_____

_____

Part 2—Market Analysis, Identity, and Communication

_____ 1. Market research is typically conducted using one of four methods and is designed to get customer feedback about product offerings.

_____

_____

_____ 2. The sampling method of market research requires restaurants to prepare sample portions of new menu items to give to customers for their comments.

_____

_____

_____ 3. The target market refers to the audience or group a business intends to pursue as customers.

_____

_____

_____ 4. Demographics refers to the way people are calculated by specific traits, such as age or geographic location.

_____

_____

_____ 5. Positioning as it applies to marketing involves the geographic location of the operation compared to its competitors.

_____

_____

_____ 6. Sales promotions are special incentives designed to bring more customers to the business.

_____

_____

Part 3—The Menu as Marketing Tool

_____ 1. The menu serves as both a planning tool and a communication tool.

_____

_____

_____ 2. An à la carte menu offers multiple menu items for one price.

_____

_____

_____ 3. A California menu is one that offers breakfast, lunch, and dinner at all times.

_____

_____

_____ 4. When creating a menu, it should take in to account the abilities of the staff and the operation's goals.

_____

_____

_____ 5. The food percentage method of pricing the menu is based on a pre-determined food cost percentage that must be achieved by the operation.

_____

_____

_____ 6. Items designated as "plow horse" items after a menu analysis should be immediately removed from the menu because of their low sales.

_____

_____

Activity 7.2
Crossword Puzzle—Marketing

Directions

Complete the following statements, and then use the answers to complete the crossword puzzle.

ACROSS

2. _____ are free or reduced-priced merchandise with the operation's name on it.

4. Operations must keep in touch with what is happening in the community. This is known as a market _____.

5. _____ involves testing a product with a specific, small group of people.

6. _____ is the process of communicating a business's message to its market.

7. _____ is the attention that an operation receives.

8. A _____ analysis is conducted by an operation to understand its current situation.

9. _____ is the act of creating a clear and specific identity for both a product and the operation within the marketplace.

10. The _____ method of research involves observing how customers react in a natural setting towards a product.

DOWN

1. _____ marketing treats everyone as wanting and needing the same things.

2. The process where an operation interacts with the public at large is known as _____ _____.

3. Market _____ is how marketers break down a large group into smaller groups of individuals with similar interests.

www.CrosswordWeaver.com

Activity 7.3
Creating a Marketing Plan

Directions

You are part of the marketing team for the Easy Street Café. The café has been in business for 10 years. During that time, the café has become known for its amazing homemade desserts; however, it also serves burgers and sandwiches and features both vegetarian and non-vegetarian daily specials. You have been asked by the general manager to create a marketing plan that will not only increase revenue at the café, but also improve the café's image with the public.

In order to create an effective marketing plan you will need to identify the following elements:

- What are the current market conditions?

- What does the café hope to accomplish in terms of increased sales and improved image?

- How will they accomplish this?

- How will they know the plan has succeeded?

Use the space below to work out the general outline, and then create a four- to five-page marketing plan that you can share with the class.

_____

_____

_____

_____

_____

_____

_____

_____

_____

_____

_____

_____

_____

_____

_____

Activity 7.4
Research Customer Habits

Directions

The owner of a local steak house has asked you to create a customer survey that can be used to gather data about three new menu items that the chef would like to introduce in the spring. To complete this task, the owner has asked that you create a paper survey (or online survey) that all guests can be given and also to create the guidelines that could be used with a focus group that will be invited to the restaurant to taste the new dishes.

Use separate sheets of paper, poster board, or your computer to create your final survey.

1. Use the space provided below to draft your survey questions.

_____

_____

_____

_____

_____

_____

_____

_____

_____

_____

2. Use the space provided to write the guidelines for a customer focus group that will taste new menu items.

_____

_____

_____

_____

_____

_____

_____

_____

_____

_____

Activity 7.5
Design a Sales Promotion for Easy Street Café

Directions

The manager of the Easy Street Café has decided that it is important to build family business during Sunday brunch. Design a sales promotion that will increase both the guest count and the average check for Sunday brunch. Keep the following information in mind as you design the promotion:

- The restaurant serves brunch on Sundays from 7:00 a.m. – 2:00 p.m.
- The current guest count for Sunday brunch is 150 guests. The restaurant can easily accommodate double or triple that amount.
- The average guest check is $12.50.

Design a coupon, social media promotion, text message campaign, or Web page to announce this new sales promotion.

Take your notes in the space below. Use a separate sheet of paper, poster board, or your computer to create your finished product.

Activity 7.6
Classroom Media Group, Inc.

Directions

You have been hired by the Easy Street Café to create an ad for them. This ad can be a print ad, radio ad, television ad, or online ad. Working as a team, create your ad using the information provided about your client.

- Restaurant location: The café is located in a strip mall surrounded by several mid-priced retail shops. The mall is busier on the weekends and during the evenings.

- Size: The café seats 100 people indoors and during warm weather can seat an additional 25 on the patio.

- Décor/Theme: The café is decorated with posters from famous movies, and the floor is black-and-white vinyl. The walls are a combination of black, white, and gray, and the inside of the restaurant features six booths and several round tables, plus six–eight square tables.

- Atmosphere: The café has an upscale, fun atmosphere where students and families can go to enjoy a delicious meal or treat.

- Staff strengths: The café staff are mainly theater majors who enjoy performing and pay attention to the details. The staff provides a high level of customer service and prides themselves on knowing the "regulars" by name.

- Menu items and specials: The café features a wide variety of burgers and sandwiches, and offers daily vegetarian and non-vegetarian specials. The café is known for its extraordinary, baked-on-premise desserts.

- Special features: Carry-out, live music on the weekends, and homemade desserts are some of the special features.

- Customer types: Customers include families, students, and office workers at lunch.

- Hours of operation: Seven days a week, serving breakfast on weekends only. Closes at 10 p.m. nightly.

Based on this information, choose one of the following options:

Option A:
Print Advertisement (newspaper, local magazine)

Using existing newspaper ads (or local magazines) as examples, design a ¼-page advertisement for your "client." Use graphics, decorative type styles, borders, catch phrases, quotes, or slogans. Each member on the team should take an active role in creating the advertisement. Possible roles for team members include:

- Creating the text
- Illustrating the ad
- Presenting the ad to the class
- Recording the team's ideas
- Creating the ad on the computer

Option B:
30-second Radio Commercial

Write, perform, and record a 30-second radio commercial for your "client" using music and/or sound effects. Each member on the team should take an active role in creating the commercial. Possible roles for team members include:

- Recording the suggestions of the team
- Writing the script
- Presenting the commercial to the class
- Providing voices
- Coordinating music/sound effects
- Writing the music

Option C:
30-second Television Commercial

Write, direct, perform, and record a 30-second commercial for your "client." Each member on the team should take an active role in creating the commercial. Possible roles for the team members include:

- Recording the suggestions of the team
- Writing the script
- Presenting the commercial to the class
- Providing voices
- Coordinating music/sound effects
- Operating the camera and editing the recording

Option D:
Web Page

Using other restaurant Web sites found online as examples, design a home page for your "client." Use whatever resources you have available or know how to use, such as graphics, decorative type, color, hyperlinks, and quotes or slogans. Each member of the team should take an active role in creating the Web site. Possible roles for team members include:

- Recording the suggestions of the team
- Creating the page layout
- Selecting the graphics and font
- Coordinating music/sound effects
- Creating the graphics
- Presenting the Web site to the class

Take your notes in the space below. Use a separate sheet of paper, poster board, or your computer to create your final product.

Activity 7.7
Conducting a SWOT analysis

Directions

The GM of the Easy Street Café has found your marketing work very good so far and has asked you to continue working on a long-term marketing project—in this case, a SWOT analysis. Using the information provided in Activity 7.6 about the Easy Street Café, perform a simple SWOT analysis. Use the space below to fill in your answers.

1. What are the strengths of the Easy Street Café?

_____

_____

_____

_____

_____

_____

_____

_____

_____

2. What are the weaknesses of the Easy Street Café?

_____

_____

_____

_____

_____

_____

_____

_____

_____

3. What are the opportunities for the Easy Street Café?

_____

_____

_____

_____

_____

_____

_____

_____

_____

_____

4. What are the threats that face the Easy Street Café?

_____

_____

_____

_____

_____

_____

_____

_____

_____

_____

Activity 7.8
Create a Menu

Directions

You have been hired as the chef for a new family-style restaurant that will be opening in town. You need to create a menu that will appeal to families in both variety and price. The layout should be easy to read, but due to budget constraints you are limited to a menu that is 8.5″ × 11″ and is on 1 piece of paper, printed front and back, that will be laminated. The same menu will be used at both lunch and dinner. Additional requirements are found here:

- Six Sections to the Menu:
  - Appetizers
  - Soups
  - Salads
  - Entrées
  - Desserts
  - Beverages
- Each section of the menu should provide at least four choices.
- Each menu item should include a description.

- Layout:
  - The menu should be easy to read, and use at least three different font sizes and types.
  - The menu should include descriptions of each item and the price.
  - The menu should have at least one picture of food for each category.
  - The menu should include the restaurant name.

Use the space provided on the following page to sketch out your menu, and then use word processing software or additional sheets of paper to create the final menu.

Activity 7.9
Menu Matching

Directions

Match each of the words and phrases listed below with its correct definition. Each letter will only be used once.

	1. Fonts	A.	Menu mix divided by total number of items sold
	2. Cover stock	B.	Advertising material attached to a menu that announces special items
	3. Plow horse	C.	Menu items with a low menu mix percentage and a high contribution margin
	4. Menu analysis	D.	Different styles of type
	5. Star	E.	Menu item with a high menu mix percentage and a low contribution margin
	6. Clip-on	F.	Menu item with low menu mix percentage and low contribution margin
	7. Puzzle	G.	Heavy cover paper
	8. Menu mix percentage	H.	Procedure that helps managers make decisions about keeping, cutting, or adding menu items
	9. Contribution margin	I.	Menu items with a high menu mix percentage and a high contribution margin
	10. Dog	J.	Portion of dollars a particular menu item contributes to the overall profits

Activity 7.10
Menu Analysis

Directions

You have been asked to conduct a menu analysis for a one-week period in June. During this time, construction was occurring, and the owner is trying to determine how the construction-crowd orders compare to the regular-lunch crowd. Complete the missing columns in the worksheet on the following page, and then answer these questions:

1. What item was the most popular on the menu during the week in consideration?

   _____

   _____

2. Which item was the least popular during this time period?

   _____

   _____

3. If you were to replace one item on the menu what would it be, and why?

   _____

   _____

   _____

   _____

   _____

   _____

   _____

   _____

Menu Analysis Worksheet

A Menu Item	B Number Sold	C Menu Mix %	D Selling Price	E Item Food Cost	F Item Contribution Margin (D-E)	G Total Revenue (B × D)	H Total Food Cost (B × E)	I Total Contribution Margin (G-H)	J Contribution Margin (High or Low)	K Menu Item Classification (Dog, Plow Horse, Puzzle, Star)
Hamburger	21	14.0	$8.00	$2.40					high	
Cheeseburger	45	30.0	$9.50	$3.16					high	
Hot Dog	26	17.3	$4.50	$1.50					low	
Grilled Cheese	5	0.03	$3.50	$1.16					low	
French Fries	45	30.0	$2.75	$0.92					high	
Peach Pie	8	0.05	$1.95	$0.65					low	
Totals	150									

Chapter **8**

Activity 8.1
Test Your Knowledge of Desserts and Baked Goods IQ

Directions

Mark each of the following statements related to desserts and baked goods as either T (True) or F (False). Rewrite the false statements to make them true.

Part 1—Bakeshop Basics

_____ 1. The main ingredients used in baking belong to one of eight different categories.

_____

_____

_____ 2. When discussing strengtheners used in baking, this refers to the structures that support a cake, such as the pillars in a wedding cake.

_____

_____

_____ 3. Sweeteners are used to provide flavor and color and include sugar, syrup, and honey.

_____

_____

_____ 4. The only type of leavening that can be used successfully in all baked goods is yeast.

_____

_____

_____ 5. Standardized recipes used in bakeries follow a different format than a regular recipe using a formula for the recipe.

_____

_____

_____ 6. The baker's percentage uses flour as 100 percent, and all other ingredients are in relationship to this item.

_____

_____

Part 2—Yeast Breads

_____ 1. Yeast is a living organism that is added to breads and pastries to make the dough rise.

_____

_____

_____ 2. In bread, making a lean dough is made with artificial sweetener and 1 percent milk to cut back the calorie content.

_____

_____

_____ 3. Rich doughs are made with ingredients such as sugar, milk, and eggs, and have a more cake-like consistency.

_____

_____

_____ 4. Dough that has been left to proof is checked by another baker to make sure the correct formula was used for the type of bread requested.

_____

_____

_____ 5. Making yeast breads can be time-consuming, requiring a 10-step process to make the bread correctly.

_____

_____

Part 3—Quick Breads and Cakes

_____ 1. Quick breads and cakes are popular snack items that require a time-consuming, multistep process to make.

_____

_____

_____ 2. Quick breads require the use of leavenings, but instead of organic leavening, such as yeast, they use chemical leavenings, which don't require time for the bread to rise.

_____

_____

_____ 3. The dough used to make quick breads and cakes is called batter and is thinner and can be poured.

_____

_____

_____ 4. In order to truly be called a cake, a rich icing must be used so that the cake is protected.

_____

_____

_____ 5. Steamed puddings are made from eggs and sugar and include items such as baked custard.

_____

_____

Part 4—Pies, Pastries, and Cookies

_____ 1. Most pies are made from cookie crust dough because they are easy to bake.

_____

_____

_____ 2. One of the most common filings used for pies is fruit; however, pies can also be filled with chocolate, nuts, or even sweet potatoes.

_____

_____

_____ 3. Pastries such as Danish are made using the roll-in dough method.

_____

_____

_____ 4. Puff pastry and phyllo doughs are both used to create a variety of pastries including baklava or cream puffs.

_____

_____

_____ 5. Cookies are a low-fat alternative to desserts such as pies and cakes and can be eaten regularly.

_____

_____

Part 5—Chocolate

_____ 1. Nibs are the basis for all cocoa products.

_____

_____

_____ 2. Chocolate liquor is a dessert beverage served with ice.

_____

_____

_____ 3. Chocolate that has a white coating, or bloom, on the surface is not safe to eat.

_____

_____

_____ 4. Tempering chocolate refers to the process of melting it by heating gently and gradually.

_____

_____

_____ 5. Tempered chocolate can be used to coat items with an even shell of chocolate that will then harden.

_____

_____

Part 6—Specialty Desserts

_____ 1. Sherbet is a type of frozen dessert made solely from fruit juice and sweeteners.

_____

_____

_____ 2. Desserts made from poached fruit combine fruit, a liquid (typically wine), sugar, and spices.

_____

_____

_____ 3. A torte is a type of layer cake.

_____

_____

_____ 4. Crème anglaise is a frosting used on tortes and brownies.

_____

_____

_____ 5. Great care should be put into creating food presentations that look pleasing to the eye.

_____

_____

Activity 8.2
Timeline—Bread through the Ages

Directions

Bread is available in a variety of forms, from sandwich bread sold in grocery stores to fresh baked rolls at a bakery or tortillas served with rice and beans. Did you know that bread has been eaten in some form since antiquity? You will be creating a bread timeline starting with 8,000 B.C. through the current day. Create a timeline focusing on key changes in bread making from early times until the present.

- Divide the timeline into four categories:
  - Ancient
  - Medieval
  - Industrial Age
  - Modern

- For each time period include the following information:
  - Types of grain used
  - Types of bread developed (include explanations and/or pictures)
  - Changes in society
  - Changes in technology
  - The future of bread

Take your notes in the space below. Use a separate sheet of paper, poster board, or your computer to create your timeline.

_____

_____

_____

_____

_____

_____

_____

_____

_____

_____

Activity 8.3
Lab—Yeast Breads

Directions

There's nothing like fresh bakery items to complement a meal. Baking is a science, and professional baking is probably much different than the baking you've done before. In order to round out your baking skills, it is important to experiment with different types of dough, flavors, and preparation methods.

Recipe Selection

- Pizza Dough
- Soft Rolls
- Whole Wheat Bread

Objectives

After completing this lab activity, you should be able to:

- Apply effective *mise en place*
- Demonstrate proper use of bakery equipment and tools
- Follow basic food safety and sanitation guidelines
- Follow basic safety guidelines to avoid causing injury to self or others
- Prepare and serve a variety of baked goods

Directions

1. Review the recipe you have been assigned.
2. Perform *mise en place*.
3. Plan for any substitutions or additional ingredients you have been given.
4. Prepare the recipe.
5. Clean the area.

Pizza Dough

Yield: 10, 8″ pizzas

Measure	Ingredients
2 tbsp	All-purpose flour
1½ c	Warm water (105°F)
1 tbsp	Honey
1 pkg (or 2¼ tsp)	Dry yeast
4 to 5 c	Bread flour
½ tsp	Salt

Directions

1. In a large bowl, whisk together the flour, warm water, honey, and yeast.

2. Allow the yeast to proof for 15 minutes, or until there is visible growth.

3. Use a wooden spoon to stir in 2 cups of bread flour and the salt.

4. Gradually add the remaining flour, as necessary, to make a stiff, elastic dough.

5. Turn the dough out onto a lightly floured board.

6. Knead the dough by hand until it is smooth and elastic, about 12 minutes.

7. Let the dough rise until it is nearly doubled in size.

8. Punch the dough down, and divide into 10 equal parts.

9. Roll the dough into balls and allow them to rest for 20–30 minutes.

10. Roll each ball into a disk about 8″ in diameter.

11. Place dough on pizza pan, top with desired ingredients, and bake at 350°F for approximately 10-12 minutes, until crust is golden brown.

Note:

1 package yeast = 2¼ teaspoons = ¼ ounce

Soft Rolls

Yield: 1 dozen rolls

Measure	Ingredients
¾ c	Whole milk
1 pkg (2¼ tsp)	Active dry yeast
¼ c	Sugar
¼ c	Shortening
1	Egg
½ tsp	Salt, kosher
2¾ c	All-purpose flour
¼ c	Butter

Directions

1. Preheat the oven to 375°F.

2. Heat ½ cup of the milk to 100°F–110°F, and add yeast. Let stand about 5 minutes.

3. Add sugar to yeast, and let stand another 2–3 minutes.

4. Combine in a separate bowl the remaining milk, shortening, egg, and salt. Whisk, and then add the yeast mixture.

5. Add flour, about a cup at a time, and mix well. After the second cup, add enough of the remaining flour to make soft dough.

6. Knead dough until smooth.

7. Place dough in a greased bowl, turning once to cover the dough with oil on all sides.

8. Cover, and let rise in a proofer or warm location until it is doubled in size.

9. Turn out dough onto a floured surface, and knead about 3 minutes.

10. Cut dough in 1½-ounce portions, and form rolls.

11. Place on a greased sheet pan, and brush with melted butter.

12. Let rise in a proofer or warm area to about double in shape.

13. Bake 15–18 minutes, or until golden brown.

14. Brush with remaining butter when the rolls come out of the oven.

If holding dough to complete another day, use the method of preparation listed below to retard the growth of the yeast and allow for great rolls even if you are limited on time.

Follow steps 1–7

8. Cover the bowl with a piece of plastic wrap, and refrigerate for up to 3 days.

9. Remove the bowl from the refrigerator, and punch down.

10. Let dough rest about 15 minutes, and then form rolls in the desired shape.

11. Place the rolls on a greased sheet, and let rise in a warm place until doubled in size.

12. Bake for 15–18 minutes, depending on size of your rolls.

Whole Wheat Bread

Yield: 1 loaf

Measure	Ingredients
1 c	Warm water (105°F)
¾ pkg	Active dry yeast
¼ c, divided	Honey
1½ c	Bread flour
1 tsp	Salt
1⅛ c	Whole wheat flour
½ tbsp	Butter, melted

Directions

1. In a large bowl, mix warm water, yeast, and ⅛ cup honey.

2. Add the bread flour, and stir to combine.

3. Let sit for 30 minutes, or until mass is big and bubbly.

4. Mix in the melted butter, ⅛ cup honey, and salt.

5. Stir in ½ of the whole wheat flour.

6. On a clean workspace, flour the surface and knead the dough mixture until just slightly sticky. The bread should pull away from the workspace, but still be a little sticky to touch.

7. If the dough is too sticky, add more whole wheat flour. When the dough is the proper texture, place in a large greased bowl.

8. Turn the mass of dough once to coat all sides, and then cover the bowl with a clean towel.

9. Let rise in a warm place until doubled in size.

10. Punch down the dough.

11. Place the dough in greased 9″ × 5″ loaf pan, and allow to rise again until the dough tops the pan by 1″.

12. Bake at 350°F for 25-30 minutes; do not overbake.

13. Brush the top of the loaf with melted butter so it doesn't harden.

14. Cool for 10 minutes in the pan, and then on a cooling rack until completely cool.

Activity 8.4
Lab—Working with Yeast

Directions

In this experiment, you will observe the role temperature plays in baking. The temperature of the ingredients can affect the quality of the dough and the way in which yeast reacts.

Follow these steps and record your observations. Before conducting the experiment, record what you think will happen. Compare your original prediction to the end result. Did you accurately predict what would happen? Why or why not?

1. Pour 1 package yeast, 1 teaspoon sugar, 2 tablespoons all-purpose flour, and 1 cup of room temperature water in each soda bottle.

2. Place 1 bottle in a saucepan filled with hot (not boiling) water.

3. Place the other bottle in a container filled with ice water.

4. Secure a balloon on top of each bottle with a rubber band.

5. Keep both containers at a constant temperature; you may have to add more hot water or ice water.

6. Record your observations.

7. Evaluate your results, and explain why the 2 containers reacted differently.

Take your notes in the space below. Present your findings to the class.

_____

_____

_____

_____

_____

_____

_____

_____

_____

_____

_____

_____

_____

Activity 8.5
Lab—Quick Breads and Cakes

Directions

Quick breads and cakes take less time to make than yeast breads and can be served with breakfast, lunch, dinner, or as a snack. Muffins and scones are often served with fruit for breakfast, while cornbread or zucchini bread might accompany dinner. Both quick breads and cakes lend themselves to change. Once the basic batters are mastered, the sky is the limit.

Recipe Selection

- Zucchini Bread

- Corn Muffins

- Cranberry Orange Walnut Scones

- Angel Food Cake

Objectives

After completing this lab activity, you should be able to:

- Apply effective *mise en place*

- Demonstrate proper use of bakery equipment and tools

- Follow basic food safety and sanitation guidelines

- Follow basic safety guidelines to avoid causing injury to self or others

- Prepare and serve a variety of quick breads

Directions

1. Review the recipe you have been assigned.

2. Perform *mise en place.*

3. Plan for any substitutions or additional ingredients you have been given.

4. Prepare the recipe.

5. Clean the area.

Zucchini Bread

Yield: 2 loaves

Measure	Ingredients
3½ c	Flour
1 tsp	Salt
2 tsp	Baking powder
½ tsp	Baking soda
½ tsp	Cinnamon, ground
½ tsp	Nutmeg, ground
¼ tsp	Cloves, ground
2 (2½ c)	Zucchini, large, peeled, and grated
1 c	Sugar
4	Eggs
½ c	Vegetable oil
1 c	Pecans/walnuts, chopped coarse, toasted (optional)

Directions

1. Preheat oven to 350°F.
2. Grease and flour 2 loaf pans.
3. Sift together the dry ingredients: flour, salt, baking powder, baking soda, cinnamon, nutmeg, and cloves.
4. Combine the zucchini, sugar, eggs, and oil in a large bowl. Mix well.
5. Stir the sifted ingredients into the zucchini mixture until the dry ingredients are blended into the batter.
6. Fold in the nuts, if included.
7. Transfer the batter into the prepared loaf pans.
8. Bake the bread in the preheated oven until fully baked, about 50–55 minutes.
9. Remove the bread from pans.
10. Cool on racks.

Corn Muffins

Yield: 16 muffins

Measure	Ingredients
As needed	Cooking spray
2 c	Cornmeal
⅔ c	Bread flour
2 tsp	Baking powder
½ tsp	Baking soda
¼ c	Sugar
1 tsp	Salt
3	Eggs
2 c	Milk or buttermilk
⅓ c	Vegetable oil

Directions

1. Preheat the oven to 350°F.
2. Line muffin tins with paper liners or spray them lightly with cooking spray.
3. Mix together the dry ingredients: cornmeal, bread flour, baking powder, baking soda, sugar, and salt.
4. Stir together the eggs, milk (or buttermilk), and oil until blended.
5. Add the wet ingredients to the dry ingredients. Combine until just mixed.
6. Pour the batter into the prepared muffin tins.
7. Bake at 350°F for 18–20 minutes or until the surface is golden brown and springs back when lightly pressed with a fingertip.
8. Slightly cool the muffins on a rack.
9. Sever while warm.

Note:

To make buttermilk, add 1¾ tablespoons of cream of tartar to a cup of milk, or add 1 tablespoon of lemon juice or white vinegar to a cup of milk and let it stand for 5 minutes.

Cranberry Orange Walnut Scones

Yield: 8

Measure	Ingredients
3 c	All-purpose flour
½ c	Sugar
5 tsp	Baking powder
½ tsp	Salt
¾ c	Butter
1	Egg
⅓ c	Milk
½ c	Orange juice, fresh
1 c	Cranberries, dried, sweetened
½ c	Walnuts, chopped coarsely (optional)

Directions

1. Preheat oven to 400°F.
2. Lightly grease a baking sheet.
3. In a large bowl, combine dry ingredients: flour, sugar, baking powder, and salt. Cut in the butter.
4. In a small bowl, mix the egg, milk, and orange juice. Stir into flour mixture until moistened.
5. Stir in the cranberries and walnuts (if included).
6. Turn the dough out on a clean, lightly floured workspace, and knead briefly.
7. Roll the dough out into a ½"-thick circle.
8. Cut into 8 pieces, and place on the prepared baking sheet.
9. Bake approximately 15 minutes, or until golden brown.

Note:

Reconstitute dried cranberries just as you would raisins, by soaking them in hot water and letting stand for 15–20 minutes. Drain off water, and then use as instructed.

Angel Food Cake

Yield: 10″ cake

Measure	Ingredients
18	Egg whites
2 tsp	Cream of tartar
1 pinch	Salt
1½ c	Sugar
1 c	Cake flour
½ c	Confectioner's sugar
2 tsp	Vanilla extract

Directions

1. Preheat oven to 350°F.

2. Sift cake flour and confectioner's sugar together 5 times.

3. In a large bowl, whip egg whites with a pinch of salt until foamy. Add cream of tartar, and continue beating until soft peaks form. Gradually add the sugar while beating until stiff peaks form. Add the vanilla.

4. Quickly fold in flour mixture.

5. Pour into a 10″ angel food (tube) pan.

6. Bake for 45 minutes, or until golden brown.

7. Turn upside down on the cooling rack to cool.

Activity 8.6
Menu Planning—Expanding the Quick Bread and Cake Offerings

Directions

The manager of the Easy Street Café has conducted some market research and found that the customers are interested in more bread and cake options on the menu. You have been asked to create a new menu that a focus group can sample and provide feedback on. The manager has asked you to include the following information on the menu:

- Three different quick breads
- Three cakes
- A description of each item along with a picture (selling point)
- A suggested selling price (research prices by visiting a local bakery or grocery store)
- Include the name of the restaurant, at least two fonts, and an eye-catching layout

On a separate piece of paper include the following information:

- The process used to make the item
- An ingredient list
- The cost to make each item
- Suggested selling price for each item (use a 30 percent suggested food cost percentage for each)

Recipe Costing Worksheet

Amount Needed	Ingredient	Cost per Unit	Total Cost (amount needed × cost per unit)
Total Cost			

Menu price: Total cost × .030 = Selling price

Take your notes in the space below. Present your findings to the class.

_____

_____

_____

_____

_____

_____

_____

_____

_____

_____

_____

_____

_____

_____

_____

_____

_____

_____

Activity 8.7
Lab—Pies, Pastries, and Cookies

Directions

The perfect dessert is an ideal way to end a meal, and choosing from a selection of pies, pastries, and cookies is always a treat. Creating the perfect dessert takes practice, but once the skills are mastered, anything is possible.

Recipe Selection

- Pie Crust
- Apple Pie
- Coconut Cream Pie
- Lemon Meringue Tart
- Marbleized Pound Cake
- Chocolate Pinwheel Cookie

Objectives

After completing this lab activity, you should be able to:

- Apply effective *mise en place*
- Demonstrate proper use of bakery equipment and tools
- Follow basic food safety and sanitation guidelines
- Follow basic safety guidelines to avoid causing injury to self or others
- Prepare and serve a variety of baked goods

Directions

1. Review the recipe you have been assigned.
2. Perform *mise en place*.
3. Plan for any substitutions or additional ingredients you have been given.
4. Prepare the recipe.
5. Clean the area.

Pie Crust

Yield: 1

Measure	Ingredients
3 lb	All-purpose flour
½ oz	Salt
2 lb	Butter, cut into pieces, chilled
16 fl oz	Water, cold

Directions

1. Combine the flour and salt thoroughly.

2. Gently rub the butter into the flour, using your fingertips to form large flakes for a very flaky crust or until it looks like coarse meal for a finer crumb.

3. Add the water all at once.

4. Mix until the dough just comes together. It should be moist enough to hold together when pressed into a ball.

5. Turn the dough out on a clean, floured work surface, and shape into an even rectangle.

6. Wrap the dough with plastic wrap, and chill for 20–30 minutes.

7. The dough is ready to roll out now, or it may be held under refrigeration for up to 3 days or frozen for up to 6 weeks.

8. Scale the dough out as necessary, using about 1 ounce of dough per 1″ of pie pan diameter.

9. To roll out the dough, work on a floured surface, and roll the dough into the desired shape and thickness, using smooth, even strokes.

10. Transfer the dough to a prepared pie pan or tart pan.

11. The shell is now ready to fill or bake blind.

Apple Pie

Yield: 9″ pie

Measure	Ingredients
1¾ lb	Pie dough
1½ lb	Golden delicious apples, peeled, cored, and sliced
5 oz	Sugar
½ oz	Tapioca starch
¾ oz	Cornstarch
½ tsp	Salt
½ tsp	Nutmeg, ground
½ tsp	Cinnamon, ground
1 tbsp	Lemon juice
1 oz	Butter, melted

Directions

1. Preheat the oven to 375°F.
2. Prepare the pie dough according to directions.
3. Divide the dough into 2 equal pieces.
4. Roll half of the dough ⅛″ thick.
5. Line the pie pan with the rolled pie dough.
6. Reserve the other half, wrapped tightly under refrigeration.
7. Toss the apples with the remaining ingredients.
8. Fill the pie shell with the apple mixture.
9. Roll out the remaining dough ⅛″ thick.
10. Place it over the filling.
11. Crimp the edges to seal.
12. Cut several vents in the top of the pie.
13. Bake at 375°F until the filling is bubbling, about 45 minutes to 1 hour.

Coconut Cream Pie

Yield: 5 pies

Measure	Ingredients
5	Baked and cooled pie shells
16 oz	Sugar, divided
4 pts	Milk
8	Egg yolks
4	Eggs, whole
5 oz	Cornstarch
1 lb	Coconut, unsweetened, untoasted
4 oz	Butter
1 oz	Vanilla extract
1 (15 oz) can	Coconut cream
As needed	Whipped cream
As needed	Toasted coconut

Directions

1. In a heavy saucepan, dissolve 8 ounces sugar in milk; bring just to a boil.

2. With a whip, beat egg yolks and whole eggs in a stainless steel bowl.

3. Sift cornstarch, remaining 8 ounces sugar, and coconut into the eggs. Beat with a whip until perfectly smooth.

4. Temper egg mixture by slowly beating in the hot milk in a thin stream.

5. Return mixture to heat, and bring to a boil, stirring constantly.

6. When mixture comes to a boil and thickens, remove from heat.

7. Stir in the butter until completely melted. Add vanilla and coconut cream. Mix until completely blended.

8. Pour into pie shells. Cool, and keep chilled.

9. Decorate chilled pies with whipped cream, using a pastry bag fitted with a star tip. Garnish with toasted coconut.

© **Michael Zema, FMP/CCE. Used with permission.**

Lemon Meringue Tart

Yield: 10″ tart

Measure	Ingredients
1	Tart shell, baked and cooled
2 pt	Water
½ lb	Sugar
4	Egg yolks
2	Eggs, whole
3 oz	Cornstarch
4 oz	Sugar
2 oz	Butter
4 oz	Lemon juice
½ lb	Egg whites
½ lb	Granulated sugar

Directions

1. Bring water and ½ pound sugar to boil in a saucepan.

2. Combine yolks, eggs, cornstarch, and 4 ounces sugar. Temper by stirring in a little bit of the hot water and sugar mixture. Add tempered egg mixture into saucepan.

3. Stir constantly until it comes to a boil. Continue boiling 2–3 minutes.

4. Remove from heat, and add butter and lemon juice.

5. Pour into shell and cool.

6. To make meringue, mix egg whites and ½ pound sugar until stiff peaks are formed.

7. Top tart with meringue, and brown in a hot oven or with a blow torch.

Marbleized Pound Cake

Yield: 6, 2-lb loaves

Measure	Ingredients
As needed	Butter or vegetable spray (for loaf pans)
3 lb, 4½ oz	Cake flour
1½ oz	Baking powder
2 lb, 5½ oz	Butter, softened
2 lb, 5½ oz	Sugar
½ oz	Salt
30	Eggs, beaten
12 oz	Chocolate, bittersweet, melted, cooled

Directions

1. Coat the loaf pans with a light film of fat, or use appropriate pan liners.

2. Sift together the flour and baking powder.

3. Cream together the butter, sugar, and salt on medium speed with the paddle attachment until the mixture is smooth and light in color, about 5 minutes. Scrape down the bowl as needed.

4. Add the eggs to the butter and sugar mixture in 3 additions.

5. Add the sifted dry ingredients, mixing on low speed until just blended. Scrape down the bowl as needed.

6. Transfer ⅓ of the batter into a separate bowl.

7. Stir the melted chocolate into the batter in the separate bowl.

8. Fold the chocolate batter into the plain batter just enough to swirl the chocolate throughout. Do not blend evenly.

9. Scale 2 pounds of batter into each prepared loaf pan.

10. Bake at 350°F until a skewer inserted near the center of a cake comes out clean, about 50 minutes.

11. Cool the cakes in the pans for a few minutes before transferring them to racks to cool completely.

Chocolate Pinwheel Cookies

Yield: 4-6 dozen

Measure	Ingredients
½ c	Shortening (solid)
½ c	Sugar
2 tsp	Vanilla extract
1	Egg yolk
1 tbsp	Milk
1½ c	All-purpose flour
½ tsp	Baking powder
½ tsp	Salt
1 (1 oz) square	Unsweetened chocolate, melted
1 tbsp	Milk
2 tbsp	Hot milk

Directions

1. Preheat oven to 375°F.

2. Cream the shortening, sugar, and vanilla until thoroughly blended. Add the egg yolk and 1 tablespoon milk.

3. In a medium bowl, sift together flour, baking powder, and salt; fold into the creamed mixture.

4. Divide dough in half, and place in 2 separate bowls.

5. Add the melted chocolate and 1 tablespoon milk to the dough in 1 bowl, and mix until thoroughly blended.

6. Chill both bowls of dough for 1½ hours.

7. Line the workspace with waxed paper, and roll out each half of the dough until they form a 10″ × 12″ rectangle. Brush the chocolate layer with hot milk, and place the plain layer of dough on top of the chocolate layer, making sure the plain layer extends beyond the chocolate layer on all sides.

8. Roll as if for a jellyroll.

9. Wrap the roll in waxed paper, and chill for 2–3 hours.

10. Slice in ⅛″ to ¼″ pieces, and place on a greased cookie sheet.

11. Bake at 375°F for 8–10 minutes, until lightly brown.

Activity 8.8
Dessert Challenge

Directions

You have been asked to create a dessert buffet for a local women's group who will be celebrating the 25th anniversary of their organization. The meeting planner has asked for 10 different desserts to be served on buffet. There will be 150 women in attendance, and some menu restrictions must be taken into consideration when designing the menu. These restrictions are:

- At least five women are on gluten-free diets.
- Seven women are vegetarians.
- Six women are allergic to nuts.
- Eight women are on low-fat diets.
- Three women are diabetic.

Your challenge is to create a menu of desserts that will provide at least one tasty treat for each guest.

Part 1

Develop the menu, and include a description of each item, being sure to highlight the special dietary restrictions that it will accommodate.

Part 2

Draw (or use a graphics program) a diagram of the buffet set-up. Be sure to include the following in the diagram:

- Dessert placement with menu description card
- Utensils needed for the dessert service
- Napkins
- Decorations for the buffet

Take your notes in the space below. Present your menu to the class.

_____

_____

_____

_____

_____

_____

Activity 8.9
Lab—Chocolate, Specialty Desserts, and Sauces

Directions

A special dessert may be the signature item that causes guests to return to your restaurant for special occasions, or it may be an item that is the talk of the town. In this lab, you will have the opportunity to try some specialty items that go beyond the traditional pie or cake.

Recipe Selection

- Chocolate Mousse
- Simple Fudge
- Poached Pears
- Sorbet
- Crème Anglaise

Objectives

After completing this lab activity, you should be able to:

- Apply effective *mise en place*
- Demonstrate proper use of equipment and tools
- Follow basic food safety and sanitation guidelines
- Follow basic safety guidelines to avoid causing injury to self or others
- Prepare and serve a variety of desserts

Directions

1. Review the recipe you have been assigned.
2. Perform *mise en place*.
3. Plan for any substitutions or additional ingredients you have been given.
4. Prepare the recipe.
5. Clean the area.

Chocolate Mousse

Yield: 10 servings

Measure	Ingredients
10 oz	Bittersweet chocolate
1½ oz	Butter
5	Eggs, separated
1 fl oz	Water
2 oz	Sugar
8 fl oz	Heavy cream, whipped

Directions

1. Combine the chocolate and butter in a heat-safe bowl, and place the bowl over a saucepan containing barely simmering water (or use a double boiler).

2. Stir the chocolate and butter until melted.

3. Combine the egg yolks with half the water and half the sugar.

4. Whisk the egg yolk mixture over a hot water bath to 145°F for 15 seconds.

5. Remove from heat.

6. Whip until cool.

7. Using a large rubber spatula, fold the egg whites into the egg yolks.

8. Fold the butter-chocolate mixture into the egg mixture.

9. Fold in the whipped cream.

10. Divide the mixture.

Chocolate Fudge

Yield: 36 pieces

Measure	Ingredients
2 c	Sugar
½ c	Cocoa
¼ tsp	Salt
1 c	Milk, whole
4 tbsp	Butter
1 tsp	Vanilla extract

Directions

1. Grease a ¼ sheet pan or an 8"- or 9"-baking pan.

2. In a large, heavy saucepan, combine the sugar, cocoa, and salt.

3. Add the milk, stir, and bring to a boil while continuing to stir. The best tool for this is a wooden spoon, as you do not want to overwork your fudge and form sugar crystals.

4. Reduce the heat and stop stirring.

5. Cook the fudge approximately 20 minutes. Allow the fudge to come up to 238°F; you will need a candy thermometer for this. Be sure to attach the thermometer to the side of the pan, and do not let it sit on the bottom.

6. Remove from heat. Add butter and vanilla extract.

7. Allow the fudge to cool about an hour (110°F); do not stir at this stage.

8. Beat the mixture with the wooden spoon until the fudge loses its shine. Do not underbeat; this will take about 15 minutes. The fudge thickens as you stir.

9. Spread into greased pan and refrigerate.

10. When solid, cut into small pieces.

Note:

If you do not have a candy thermometer, another great way to tell if the fudge is ready is to drop a small drop of the fudge into cold water. When it does not fall apart, but forms a soft ball, then it is at the softball stage. (The ball should flatten easily in your fingers when it is ready.)

Poached Pears

Yield: 4 servings

Measure	Ingredients
4	Pears
1¼ c	Water
¾ c	Sugar
1 tsp	Vanilla extract

Directions

1. Peel the pears. Cut them in half, and remove cores with a melon baller.

2. Combine the water and sugar in a large saucepot. Bring to a boil, stirring until the sugar is dissolved.

3. Remove from heat, and add vanilla.

4. Add pears to the syrup and simmer very slowly until just tender, approximately 15-25 minutes.

5. Allow pears to cool in syrup. When cool, refrigerate until needed for service.

Fruit Sorbet

Yield: Approximately 2 quarts

Measure	Ingredients
2 c	Raspberries, fresh
2 c	Strawberries, fresh
½ c	Sugar
1–1½ cups	Grape juice, sparkling white

Directions

1. Place 2 cups of raspberries in a mesh strainer, and press them with the back of a spoon against the side of the strainer to squeeze out the juice. Place the strainer in a large bowl in order to capture the juices.

2. Discard the pulp and seeds.

3. Combine the raspberry juice, strawberries, and sugar in an electric blender. Cover, and blend until smooth.

4. Scrape the sides as needed.

5. Combine the fruit purée and the grape juice.

6. Pour into a tightly sealed container, and freeze for at least 2 hours.

7. To serve, scoop the frozen mixture into cups, and garnish with fresh fruit.

Crème Anglaise

Yield: About 2½ pints

Measure	Ingredients
1	Vanilla bean or 1 tbsp liquid vanilla
12	Egg yolks
8 oz	Sugar
1 qt	Milk, whole (or half and half)

Directions

1. If using vanilla bean, microwave 10–15 seconds to plump.

2. Whip egg yolks and sugar to ribbon stage.

3. Place milk (or half and half) and vanilla bean in medium saucepan. (If using liquid vanilla, you will add this later.) Heat just to boiling; be careful not to overheat.

4. Remove from heat, and whisk a few tablespoons of the milk mixture into the egg yolks to temper. Then, gradually add the remaining milk mixture, whisking constantly.

5. Return the egg/milk mixture to a medium saucepan, and gently heat until just below boiling (approximately 170-175°F). Do not boil or the eggs will curdle. You should notice steam start to appear, and the mixture will look slightly thicker than heavy cream.

6. When the custard is cooked, immediately remove from the heat, and pour through a chinois, scraping up any thickened cream that remains on the bottom of the pan.

7. Remove the vanilla bean, and scrape the seeds into the sauce. Stir until the seeds separate. If using vanilla extract instead of the vanilla bean, add it now.

Note:

If using half and half, increase sugar by 2 oz.

If crème anglaise breaks, place in food processor, and stir in about 2 tbsp cold milk.

Activity 8.10
Lab—Chocolate Molds

Directions

In this activity, you will learn to work with chocolate molds to create chocolate decorations.

Follow these steps closely. Remember to handle chocolate with care. Do not burn or scorch the chocolate or the end product will be ruined.

1. Melt your chocolate. Depending on the type of mold, you may want to use more than one color. For example, if creating milk chocolate flowers, you may want to also melt some white chocolate, and then add a little bit of food coloring to paint the mold with a splash of color.

2. Melt some white chocolate, and add food coloring to create a color to use as the first color of the mold. Paint a thin layer of this color in the appropriate section of the mold (optional).

3. Melt the chocolate. Use a double boiler or carefully melt in a microwave. The chocolate should be of a smooth consistency; be careful not to burn it.

   Note: If using real chocolate instead of chocolate coating, it must be tempered at this point.

4. Pour the chocolate into the molds. This can be done using a spoon or a measuring cup with a pouring tip.

5. Freeze the molds until the outer edges start to get solid.

   Note: If you leave the chocolate in too long, it will crack when removing from the mold and will not hold a filling.

6. Optional: If you want to create a layered chocolate item, partially fill the mold in step 4, freeze, and then repeat step 4 using an additional color/layer. Freeze again.

7. Remove the chocolate from the mold, and use as a decoration on a cake or create a chocolate platter for service.

Chapter **9**

Activity 9.1
Test Your Knowledge of Sustainability IQ

Directions

Mark each of the following statements related to sustainability as either T (True) or F (False). Rewrite the false statements to make them true.

Part 1—Water Conservation

_____ 1. The Environmental Protection Agency (EPA) was founded in 1816 and was created to regulate mining and coal production.

_____

_____

_____ 2. Sustainability refers to practices designed to meet resource needs without compromising the ability to meet future needs.

_____

_____

_____ 3. Conservation is the practice of using resources until they are almost exhausted and then finding an alternative.

_____

_____

_____ 4. There are several steps restaurants can take to help control water consumption; one of these is to pre-wash dishes before sending them through the dishwasher.

_____

_____

_____ 5. A low-flow spray valve is designed to limit the amount of water coming out of a sink sprayer.

_____

_____

_____ 6. A connectionless steamer uses 90 percent more water than a traditional steamer, but takes up less space in the kitchen, making it a good investment.

_____

_____

Part 2—Energy Conservation

_____ 1. Fossil fuels are considered non-renewable resources and include natural gas, coal, and petroleum.

_____

_____

_____ 2. Renewable energy sources are those that do not rely on a limited supply of a resource and include water and wind.

_____

_____

_____ 3. Hydropower comes from harnessing the heat inside the earth and using steam or hot water to heat buildings.

_____

_____

_____ 4. Utility costs consume approximately 25–34 percent of a restaurant's total-annual sales.

_____

_____

_____ 5. EnergyStar is a program from the EPA and the U.S. Department of Energy that provides free, online tracking programs to compare month-to-month energy usage.

_____

_____

_____ 6. A green building is one that has been designed or renovated so the building conserves energy and uses resources more efficiently.

_____

_____

Part 3—Waste Management

_____ 1. Repurposed food is food that was prepared by the kitchen but customers did not eat. The food is then reused in another manner.

_____

_____

_____ 2. There are many ways to reduce waste in the operation; two steps that operators can take to reduce waste are using biodegradable dinnerware and buying furniture made from recycled materials.

_____

_____

_____ 3. Many companies choose not to recycle because it's difficult and there are few items that can easily be recycled.

_____

_____

_____ 4. Composting is a natural form of recycling that uses organic materials and turns them into fertilizer.

_____

_____

_____ 5. Coffee grounds, waxed paper, and tea bags should not be composted because they may attract pests and cause a bad odor.

_____

_____

_____ 6. Putting a composting plan in place is a relatively simple process for a restaurant to implement.

_____

_____

Part 4—Sustainable Food Practices

_____ 1. A local source offers food produced in the local area.

_____

_____

_____ 2. Food miles refer to the distance food must travel from grower to consumer.

_____

_____

_____ 3. Aquaculture is the production of seafood in the wild.

_____

_____

_____ 4. Aquaculture refers to the farmed fish industry and has blossomed since 1970, producing over 45 million tons of seafood annually.

_____

_____

_____ 5. Shade-grown coffee is coffee grown using newer methods that require strict plant management and extensive use of fertilizers and pesticides.

_____

_____

_____ 6. Restaurants can apply for organic certification through the USDA's National Organic Program.

_____

_____

Activity 9.2
Crossword Puzzle—Sustainability and the Foodservice Industry

Directions

Complete the following statements, and then use the answers to complete the crossword puzzle.

ACROSS

2. A natural form of recycling that uses organic material is called _____.

6. Fuels that are formed from plant or animal remains that have been buried deep in the earth are called _____ _____.

9. Energy sources that can be replenished quickly are known as _____ energy sources.

10. Energy that comes from directing, harnessing, or channeling moving water is referred to as _____.

11. _____ refers to the production of seafood under controlled conditions.

14. _____ occurs when some species of fish are caught faster than they can reproduce.

15. _____ offers environmental benefits and helps to prevent pollution, reduce greenhouse gases, and save energy.

16. The amount of travel that food products must make from the source to their final destination is known as _____ _____.

DOWN

1. _____ _____ is food that customers did not eat, but that was prepared by the kitchen.

3. _____ refers to the practices that meet current resource needs without compromising the ability to meet future needs.

4. _____ energy is produced from the heat inside the earth.

5. _____ is the practice of limiting the use of a resource.

7. _____ is an acronym for Leadership in Energy and Environment Design, and it certifies that a contractor or architect has been trained to create environmentally friendly buildings.

8. Solar cells that can convert sunlight directly into electricity are also known as _____ cells.

12. Fishing boats that pull large nets through the water are known as _____.

13. An _____ adds air to water flow, and they are frequently used in sinks.

www.CrosswordWeaver.com

Activity 9.3
Water Conservation Plan

Directions

The mayor of your town has approached your team and asked you to create a water-conservation ad campaign. The mayor is concerned that too many restaurants are not using water wisely, and the meteorologists are predicting one of the worst droughts of the decade. Create a flyer that can be distributed to employees to help them be more aware of their water usage, and also create a 30-second public service announcement.

Use the material in your text to help you explore water-conservation ideas, and also refer to the Internet, science books, and local resources in your community.

Take your notes in the space below. Present your flyer and ad to the class.

_____

_____

_____

_____

_____

_____

_____

_____

_____

_____

_____

_____

_____

_____

_____

_____

_____

_____

_____

Activity 9.4
Lab—Cooking with Organics

Directions

Cooking with organic food items can be slightly more expensive, but many customers seek out these types of dishes.

Recipe Selection

- Minestrone Soup
- Organic Chili with Beef and Beans
- Fresh from the Garden Salad
- Strawberry Rhubarb Cobbler

Objectives

After completing this lab activity, you should be able to:

- Apply effective *mise en place*
- Demonstrate proper use of equipment and tools
- Follow basic food safety and sanitation guidelines
- Follow basic safety guidelines to avoid causing injury to self or others
- Prepare and serve a variety of dishes using organic ingredients

Directions

1. Review the recipe you have been assigned.
2. Perform *mise en place*.
3. Plan for any substitutions or additional ingredients you have been given.
4. Prepare the recipe.
5. Clean the area.

Minestrone Soup

Yield: 12 servings

Measure	Ingredients
3 c	Pasta, whole wheat pasta (spirals, wagon wheels, etc.)
5 c	Chicken broth, organic
4 oz	Tomato paste
1 c	Kidney beans, cooked
1 c	Garbanzo beans
⅓ c	Onions, chopped
½ c	Carrot, shredded
2 c	Summer squash, shredded
½ c	Asparagus
½ c	Celery, chopped
½ c	Parsley, minced
2 large	Tomatoes, chopped
1 c	Peas, frozen or fresh
3 cloves	Garlic, minced
1	Bay leaf
½ tsp	Black pepper, ground
½ tsp	Basil
½ tsp	Italian seasoning
1 tbsp	Butter
As needed	Parmesan cheese, grated

Directions

1. Wash and chop all vegetables.

2. In a Dutch oven, melt the butter, and sauté the vegetables and garlic over medium heat.

3. Add beans, broth, tomato paste, and seasoning. Simmer for 20 minutes.

4. Add precooked pasta, and simmer another 10–15 minutes, until thoroughly heated.

5. Top with freshly grated Parmesan cheese.

Note:

Where possible, use locally grown, organic produce.

Organic Chili with Beef and Beans

Yield: 12 Servings

Measure	Ingredients
3 lb	Ground beef, organic, lean
2 c	Onions, finely chopped
2 tbsp	Garlic, minced
3	Jalapeño peppers, finely chopped
1 (15 oz) can	Pinto or kidney beans, drained
1 (16 oz) can	Refried beans
3 c	Vegetable juice, spicy
24 oz	Tomato juice
2½ oz	Chili seasoning
2 tsp	Cumin, ground
¼ tsp	Cayenne pepper
To taste	Salt

Directions

1. In a large skillet, brown the beef. If necessary, separate into 3 batches. Place the beef in a large stockpot.

2. When the beef is browned, using the same skillet, add the onions, and sauté for 3 minutes. Add the garlic and peppers. Continue cooking until the onions are soft.

3. Add the onion mixture to the beef.

4. Stir in the beans, juices, chili seasoning, cumin, and cayenne. Bring to a boil, stirring occasionally. Reduce heat to low, and simmer, stirring occasionally for about 2 hours until it has thickened.

5. Add salt to taste.

5. Serve hot, or refrigerate and reheat the next day.

Note:

Where possible, use organic, locally grown ingredients.

Fresh from the Garden Salad

Yield: 4 servings

Measure	Ingredients
2 c	Vegetables, fresh, in-season (asparagus, beans, cucumbers, zucchini, etc.)
1½ c	Tomatoes, coarsely chopped
½ c	Organic cheese, diced
¼ c	Onions, sweet, sliced thin
¼ c	Olive oil, extra virgin
To taste	Herbs, fresh, chopped (basil, cilantro, mint)
2 tsp	Garlic, minced, mashed
To taste	Salt
To taste	Pepper
5–6 c	Bread, cut in cubes, slightly stale

Directions

1. Toss all the ingredients together, except the bread.

2. Refrigerate for 30 minutes.

3. Toss in bread cubes, and serve immediately.

Note:

Where possible, use locally grown, organic produce.

Strawberry Rhubarb Cobbler

Yield: 8 servings

Measure	Ingredients
1 lb	Rhubarb, fresh or frozen, chopped
3 c	Strawberries, fresh, sliced
¾ c	Sugar
2 tbsp	Flour
1 tbsp	Orange zest, grated
1¼ c	Flour
2 tbsp	Sugar
¾ tsp	Baking powder
¼ tsp	Baking soda
½ tsp	Salt
5 tbsp	Butter, organic
½ c	Sour cream, organic
3 tbsp	Soy milk, organic

Directions

1. Preheat oven to 375°F.

2. In a large bowl, combine rhubarb, strawberries, sugar, and flour. Let sit for 15 minutes, tossing occasionally.

3. For the dough topping: sift flour, sugar, baking powder, baking soda, and salt in a medium bowl. Cut in butter until sunflower-seed-size bits are formed.

4. In a small bowl, whisk together sour cream and soy milk. Pour this over the flour mixture, and stir until just combined.

5. On a clean, lightly-floured surface, place the dough topping, and knead 4–6 times. Roll into a round shape, approximately ½″ thick.

6. Using a biscuit cutter, cut the dough into biscuit rounds.

7. Gather the scraps, roll out, and repeat cutting until 8 rounds total are cut.

8. In a 9″ × 9″ square pan, spread the fruit mixture.

9. Top the fruit mixture with the biscuit rounds.

10. Bake for 40–50 minutes, until the top is golden brown and the fruit is bubbly.

Note:

Where possible, use locally grown, organic produce and dairy products.

Activity 9.5
Webquest—Energy Conservation

Directions

You will be participating in a Webquest, a virtual Easter egg hunt. Use the space provided to answer the questions about energy conservation as you explore the following Web sites. You will be provided with the URLs for this Webquest, and you will need to provide answers to the questions about each site.

Fossil Fuels and Alternative Fuels

http://www.energyquest.ca.gov/story/chapter08.html

Find the movie room, watch the video about wind power, and then answer the following question:

1. What happened on August 14, 2003, in New York City?

_____

_____

_____

_____

_____

_____

_____

Find the chapter in the energy story that explains fossil fuels and answer the following questions:

1. Why is the Carboniferous Period important to understand when studying fossil fuels?

_____

_____

_____

_____

_____

_____

_____

2. Besides being used as fuel, what other things has oil been used for throughout history? Give at least two examples.

_____

_____

_____

_____

_____

_____

_____

Renewable Energy Sources

http://www.nrel.gov/learning/re_basics.html

1. How does a wind turbine work?

_____

_____

_____

_____

_____

_____

_____

2. Outline how sunlight is converted into electricity.

_____

_____

_____

_____

_____

_____

_____

20 Things You Can Do to Conserve Energy

http://www.ecomall.com/greenshopping/20things.htm

1. What are two things that can be done at home to conserve energy when using home appliances? How can these same principles be applied to a foodservice operation? What differences are there between home energy conservation and conservation in a business?

_____

_____

_____

_____

_____

_____

_____

2. What are some items that can be replaced in the home to increase energy savings and/or decrease energy consumption? Applying the information you learned about home energy consumption, what are some items that can be replaced in the foodservice operation to decrease energy consumption?

_____

_____

_____

_____

_____

_____

3. What is one thing a foodservice operator can do in the community to help conserve energy?

_____

_____

_____

_____

_____

_____

Activity 9.6
Research Energy-Efficient Equipment

Directions

After graduating from college, you plan to open your own 75-seat restaurant. Your restaurant will offer fresh seafood, chicken, pasta, and a variety of vegetables. There will also be a children's menu that will include French fries and grilled-cheese sandwiches. For this project you will complete three parts.

Part 1

Design your menu. Create the menu and a list of cooking techniques that will be used to make the food items. The menu should be limited to 20 total items, not counting beverages. Create a spreadsheet or table to display this information.

Part 2

Develop a list of cooking equipment that will be needed to create the items on the menu.

Part 3

Visit a restaurant-equipment Web site, and research the costs of the equipment that you will need. Then, visit the Energy Star Web site (http://www.energystar.gov/) to compare the anticipated cost savings using Energy Star-approved equipment compared to equipment that is not Energy Star-approved. Write a brief summary of the anticipated benefits from using energy efficient equipment.

Take your notes in the space below. Use separate sheets of paper, poster board, or your computer to create your project.

_____

_____

_____

_____

_____

_____

_____

_____

_____

_____

Activity 9.7
Food Additives and Sustainability

Directions

Food additives are used to preserve the shelf life of food, make them more appealing, or help them survive the transportation process from one part of the globe to another. In this activity, you will be researching the different types of additives that are used in foods and then converting a recipe that uses foods with additives into one that can be made from sustainable products with the use of few additives.

Part 1

Gather the food labels from several packages of processed foods that you would eat on a regular day. (This could include soft drinks, frozen meals, canned vegetables, etc.) You can find the labels directly on the food packages, or look up the labels online.

Create a spreadsheet or table and record the following information:

- Ingredient name
- Type of additive (indirect, direct, or color)
- Use in the product

Compare your results to those of your classmates, and then select two of the additives and research what function they play in the food and why they might be added to food.

Part 2

Using the list of process foods that you selected, create a recipe that could be made using sustainable (or locally-grown foods). For example, if you selected frozen French fries, you would use fresh potatoes, salt, and oil to create handmade fries. Another example would be changing a cobbler using canned pie filling to a recipe that uses locally-grown fresh produce.

Write the recipe for the item using foods with additives, and then rewrite the recipe using sustainable-food products.

Prepare the recipes, and compare and contrast the differences in taste, texture, and flavor in addition to the nutritional value.

Use separate sheets of paper, poster board, or your computer to create your project.

Activity 9.8
Design a Recycling Plan

Directions

The manager of the Easy Street Café conducted a waste audit and realized that the café was generating too much waste each month. She has asked you to create a recycling plan for the restaurant. She has explained the goals of the recycling plan are to reduce waste and to bring in some additional revenue to the restaurant by selling the recycled items to the appropriate vendors. Create a recycling plan for the restaurant that addresses the following items:

- Which items that the restaurant uses can be recycled?
  - Food items?
  - Paper items?
  - Glass items?
  - Metal items?
- How will the items be recycled?
  - Create a special recycling area?
  - Create a new recycling position?
  - Hire a company to recycle?
- What benefits will there be to the restaurant by implementing a recycling program?
- What potential benefits will there be to the community by implementing a recycling program?
- What are some challenges the restaurant will face when beginning to implement a recycling program?
- What are the potential costs of starting a recycling program?

Take your notes in the space below. Use separate sheets of paper, poster board, or your computer to create your project.

_____

_____

_____

_____

_____

_____

_____

_____

_____

Activity 9.9
Create a Sustainable Menu

Directions

The Easy Street Café will be experimenting with some new menu options and is considering a "Sustainable Sunday" promotion. Every Sunday during the month of July, they will offer three entrées, three desserts, and three appetizers made completely with organic, locally grown, and sustainable foods. The chef has asked you to create this menu for him. Using your knowledge of menu-layout design and what you have learned about sustainable foods, create three three-course meals. The chef will need the following information from you:

- Menu items and brief descriptions
- Recipes for one of the meals

Each meal should include a soup or salad option, an entrée with a starch and vegetable, and a dessert.

Take your notes in the space below. Use separate sheets of paper, poster board, or your computer to create your menu.

_____

_____

_____

_____

_____

_____

_____

_____

_____

_____

_____

_____

_____

_____

_____

_____

_____

_____

Chapter **10**

Activity 10.1
Test Your Knowledge of Global Cuisines—
The Americas IQ

Directions

Mark each of the following statements related to global cuisine as either true (T) or false (F). Rewrite the false statements to make them true.

Part 1—North America

_____ 1. Boiled meals, such as Yankee pot roast, can present a food safety hazard if the temperatures are not brought up to a safe range quickly enough.

_____

_____

_____ 2. Typical foods from the Midwest are smoky and spicy.

_____

_____

_____ 3. Cajun cooking is associated with Louisiana, but was originally developed by French Acadian Catholics.

_____

_____

_____ 4. Southwestern cuisine was heavily influenced by the French and Italians.

_____

_____

_____ 5. In Hawaii, SPAM is served in quick-service restaurants, such as McDonald's®, and is a local classic.

_____

_____

_____ 6. A mole is a classic Mexican sauce that is often made from chocolate.

_____

_____

Part 2—Central America and the Caribbean

_____ 1. A *curtido* is a Central America relish made from tomatoes, peppers, cilantro, and other spices.

_____

_____

_____ 2. Tamales made in Central America can be steamed in either corn husks or banana leaves.

_____

_____

_____ 3. Yuca is made from the root of the cassava plant and is the same thing as tapioca and manioc.

_____

_____

_____ 4. A *cubano* is a complex dish composed of pork, peppers, cheese, spices, and mole sauce served over a bed of rice.

_____

_____

_____ 5. *Sofrito* is used as a foundation for soups and stews, and is made of salt pork, ham, onions, garlic, green peppers, jalapeños, tomato, oregano, and cilantro.

_____

_____

_____ 6. Barbecue originated in the Caribbean and spread to other parts of the world as a popular cooking method.

_____

_____

Part 3— South America

_____ 1. Unlike many other South American countries, Brazilian cuisine focuses on tropical fruits such as bananas.

_____

_____

_____ 2. Churrasco is a Brazilian specialty of meat simmered for hours in a pot of highly spiced broth.

_____

_____

_____ 3. A typical Brazilian breakfast consists of a cup of yerba matè tea, pastries, eggs, sausage, and grilled bananas.

_____

_____

_____ 4. Ceviche is a Peruvian specialty made of fish and citrus.

_____

_____

_____ 5. Cherimoya is a type of fruit rich in vitamin C that tastes like bananas, pineapples, apples, berries, and custard all in one.

_____

_____

_____ 6. The potato originated in Ireland and was carried to Peru by explorers.

_____

_____

Activity 10.2
The "Great" Food Debate

Directions

People throughout the United States are passionate about their food. A few particular types of food lead to great debates by residents from each particular region. Three of the hottest food debates are:

- Chicago vs. New York-style Pizza
- Hot Dog Styles
- Dry Rub vs. Wet Barbecue

Research one of the three topics, and either write a two- to three-page paper, create a PowerPoint presentation, or create a Web site that describes:

- The cause of the food conflict
- The differences in styles
- Where to find a representative "best" example of that food

Include pictures or recipes for additional reference or to highlight the differences between the products.

Take your notes in the space below. Use a separate sheet of paper, poster board, or your computer to create your final presentation.

_____

_____

_____

_____

_____

_____

_____

_____

_____

_____

_____

_____

_____

_____

Activity 10.3
Clambake

Directions

You have been asked by the catering manager of a large hotel to recreate a clambake for a group of guests who are at the hotel for a convention. The guests are tour-bus operators from around the world, and each region of the United States has the opportunity to showcase a regional food specialty.

The catering manager needs a brochure that will detail the following items:

- The history of the clambake
- A typical clambake menu
- How to cook the food at a clambake
- What makes a clambake special

Be sure to include pictures, as the goal is to "sell" the New England region to these tour operators. Take your notes in the space below. Use a separate sheet of paper, poster board, or your computer to create your brochure.

_____

_____

_____

_____

_____

_____

_____

_____

_____

_____

_____

_____

_____

_____

_____

_____

_____

Activity 10.4
Crossword Puzzle—Global Cuisines: The Americas

Directions

Complete the following statements, and then use the answers to complete the crossword puzzle.

ACROSS

1. _____ _____ means "painted chicken," but is actually made of white rice and black beans.

4. Chef _____ _____ popularized fusion cuisine.

6. _____ cookery was developed in the city of New Orleans in the homes of French and Spanish land owners.

8. This spicy rice dish served with chicken, andouille sausage, shrimp, crayfish, trinity and other vegetables, herbs, and broth is known as _____.

9. A Central American relish made from cabbage, onions, carrots, and vinegar is _____.

11. In _____-_____ cookery, the meat is shredded instead of ground.

14. _____ cuisine was influenced by Native Americans who taught European settlers how to plant corn and introduced them to many things, including berries, fish, and oysters.

16. A hearty soup made of trinty and shrimp and thickened with a brown roux containing okra is known as _____.

20. San Francisco is famous for _____ bread.

21. A food sweetener that comes from the _____ plant.

22. _____ is a signature dish of the Southwest and is usually a chunky sauce.

23. _____ spice is a spicy dry rub used to preserve meat and used as a Jamaican seasoning.

24. _____ is a local favorite in Hawaii, created by the Hormel company.

DOWN

2. A dried poblano pepper is called an _____ pepper.

3. This agricultural system created by the Iroquois cultivated corn, beans, and squash and is known as _____ _____.

5. Food from the Midwest is sometimes called _____ food because it is simple and filling.

7. _____ is an ancient food-science breakthrough and is the by-product of corn.

10. _____ comes from the goosefoot plant and can be ground into flour.

11. The _____ cooking method was introduced by Native Americans and finds fish, corn, and vegetables cooked in a pit made in wet sand.

12. _____ a popular bean stew in Portugal and Brazil.

13. A _____ _____ is a deep-fried mashed potato dumpling filled with ground beef, raisins, onions, and spicy hot peppers.

15. A stuffed pan-fried corn biscuit that looks like a fat homemade tortilla and is popular in Guatemala is called a _____.

17. A _____ is a round, flat griddle made of stone to cook tortillas.

18. _____ is a form of mirepoix used in Cajun and Creole cuisines.

19. A _____ is a soup made from lobster shells that have had all the flavor and color extracted.

Activity 10.5
Lab—Cuisine of North America

Directions

Each region of North America has unique foods and culinary traditions associated with the area. Discover some of the many flavors of the continent.

Recipe Selection

- New England Clam Chowder
- Macaroni and Cheese
- Chicken and Sausage Gumbo
- Barbecue Chicken Texas Style
- Hawaiian Coconut Pudding
- Chicken Pot Pie

Objectives

After completing this lab activity, you should be able to:

- Apply effective *mise en place*
- Demonstrate proper use of equipment and tools
- Follow basic food safety and sanitation guidelines
- Follow basic safety guidelines to avoid causing injury to self or others
- Prepare and serve a variety of North American dishes

Directions

1. Review the recipe you have been assigned.
2. Perform *mise en place.*
3. Plan for any substitutions or additional ingredients you have been given.
4. Prepare the recipe.
5. Clean the area.

New England Clam Chowder

Yield: 3.5 quarts

Measure	Ingredients
2 qt	Canned clams with juice
1½ qt	Water or fish stock
1 lb, 4 oz	Potatoes, small dice
8 oz	Salt pork, small dice
2 oz	Butter
1 lb	Onions, small dice
8 oz	Celery, small dice
4 oz	Flour
1 qt	Milk
8 fl oz	Heavy cream
To taste	Salt
To taste	Pepper
To taste	Hot sauce
To taste	Worcestershire sauce
To taste	Fresh thyme
As needed	Fresh parsley, for garnish
As needed	Carrot, julienned, for garnish

Directions

1. Drain the clams, reserving both the clams and their liquid. Add enough water or stock so that the total liquid equals 2 quarts.

2. Simmer the potatoes in the clam liquid until nearly cooked through. Strain, and reserve the potatoes and the liquid.

3. Render the salt pork with the butter. Add the onions and the celery to the rendered fat, and sweat until tender but not brown.

4. Add the flour, and cook to make a blonde roux.

5. Add the clam liquid to the roux, whisking away any lumps.

6. Simmer for 30 minutes, skimming as needed.

7. Bring the milk and cream to a boil and add to soup.

8. Add the clams and potatoes, and season to taste with salt, pepper, hot sauce, Worcestershire sauce, and thyme.

9. Garnish each serving with fresh parsley and julienned carrot, as desired.

Macaroni and Cheese

Yield: 6 servings

Measure	Ingredients
1 pkg (16 oz)	Macaroni, uncooked
1 tbsp	Butter
1 lb	Cheddar cheese, sharp, sliced
12 fl oz	Evaporated milk
To taste	Salt
To taste	Pepper

Directions

1. Preheat oven to 350°F.

2. Bring a large pot of salted water to a boil.

3. Add the macaroni and return to a boil.

4. Cook the macaroni until al dente, about 7–9 minutes. Do not overcook.

5. Drain the pasta, and shock in cold water to stop cooking.

6. Grease a 2-quart casserole dish.

7. Place ¼ of the macaroni into the bottom of the dish.

8. Layer ¼ of the cheddar cheese evenly on top of the macaroni.

9. Dot with butter, and season with salt and pepper to taste.

10. Repeat to create three layers of macaroni and cheese.

11. Pour the evaporated milk evenly over the top layer.

12. Bake, uncovered, for 1 hour, or until the top is golden brown.

Chicken and Sausage Gumbo

Yield: 8 servings

Measure	Ingredients
12 c	Water
3 lb	Chicken parts
12 oz	Okra, frozen
1 stick	Butter
½ c	All-purpose flour
1 lb	Andouille sausage (or other spicy sausage)
1 can (28 oz)	Tomatoes, Italian-style, whole, peeled
1	Green bell pepper, medium dice
2 stalks	Celery, medium dice
2 cloves	Garlic, minced
1	Bay leaf
2 tsp	Salt
1 tsp	Thyme, dried
1 tsp	Basil, dried
1 tsp	Cayenne pepper
1 tsp	Black pepper
1 tsp	Filé powder

Directions

1. Combine the water and chicken in a large pot, and bring to a boil.

2. Reduce heat and simmer until chicken is tender (about 1 hour).

3. Remove chicken from the water, and place in strainer. Let cool, and then remove meat from the bones.

4. Reserve the cooking liquid.

5. Melt butter in a large Dutch oven, and then add the flour, stirring constantly until it becomes a golden brown.

6. Add 4 cups of the reserved chicken broth, okra, sausage, whole tomatoes with the juice, bell pepper, celery, garlic, bay leaf, salt, thyme, basil, cayenne pepper, and black pepper. Partially cover pot, and simmer for 1½ hours or until thickened.

7. If there is any fat on the surface, spoon it off.

8. Add the chicken and filé powder to the gumbo mixture, and simmer for 15 minutes.

9. Serve over steaming white rice.

Barbecue Chicken Texas Style

Yield: 8 servings

Measure	Ingredients
8	Chicken breasts, boneless, skinless
3 tbsp	Brown sugar
1 tbsp	Paprika, ground
1 tsp	Salt
1 tsp	Dry mustard
½ tsp	Chili powder
¼ c	White vinegar
⅛ tsp	Cayenne pepper
2 tbsp	Worcestershire sauce
1½ c	Tomato juice
½ c	Ketchup
¼ c	Water
2 cloves	Garlic, minced

Directions

1. Preheat oven to 350°F.

2. In a baking dish, place the chicken breasts in a single layer.

3. In a medium bowl, combine the brown sugar, paprika, salt, dry mustard, chili powder, vinegar, cayenne pepper, Worcestershire sauce, tomato juice, ketchup, water, and garlic. Stir until combined.

4. Pour the sauce over the chicken breasts.

5. Bake uncovered for 35 minutes, or until chicken is cooked through.

6. Remove the chicken from the pan, and shred, using a fork, into a medium bowl. Return shredded chicken to the baking dish with the sauce.

7. Return the chicken and sauce to the oven, and bake for an additional 10 minutes.

Hawaiian Coconut Pudding

Yield: 8″ × 8″ pan

Measure	Ingredients
2 c	Coconut milk
1 c	Whole milk
6 tbsp	Granulated sugar
5 tbsp	Cornstarch
½ tsp	Vanilla extract
As needed	Shredded coconut

Directions

1. In a small saucepan, pour 1 cup of coconut milk.

2. In a small bowl, combine sugar and cornstarch. Stir the sugar mixture into the coconut milk. Add vanilla.

3. Stir the coconut milk, sugar, cornstarch, and vanilla mixture over low heat until thickened.

4. When mixture has thickened, stir in the remaining cup of coconut milk and the whole milk. Continue stirring until thickened.

5. Pour the mixture into an 8″-square pan, and refrigerate until firm.

6. Cut into 2″ squares, and serve on chilled plates.

7. Garnish with shredded coconut.

Chicken Pot Pie

Yield: 4 individual pies

Measure	Ingredients
1 each	Yellow onion, small
2 cloves	Garlic
1 cup	Carrot
1 cup	Celery
1 cup	Potato
1 cup	Butternut squash
3 tbsp	Oil or butter
¼ cup	Flour
½ tsp	Salt
¼ tsp	Fresh ground black pepper
3 cups	Chicken broth
3 cups	Cooked chicken meat
2 tbsp	Parsley
1 cup	Frozen green peas
1 cup	Shredded cheddar cheese
Dough for 2, 9″ piecrusts or frozen puff pastry	

Directions

1. Preheat oven to 350°F.
2. Dice onion.
3. Mince garlic.
4. Dice carrots, celery, and potatoes.
5. Sauté onions in butter until translucent; add garlic.
6. Add flour, salt, and pepper, and cook about 2 minutes, forming a roux.
7. Slowly stir in chicken broth, and bring to a boil. Immediately lower the temperature so it is at a simmer. Cook until the filling has thickened.
8. Add diced carrots, diced celery, and diced potatoes, and cook until done, about 15 minutes.
9. Remove from heat and add peas, chicken, and parsley.
10. Season with additional salt and pepper, if necessary.
11. Place filling into individual dishes lines with piecrust.
12. Sprinkle shredded cheddar cheese on top.
13. Cover dish with another piece of piecrust, and pinch edges to seal.
14. Make several cuts in the top to allow for venting.
15. Bake at 350°F until pastry is golden brown, about 25 to 35 minutes depending on the size of your dishes.
16. Serve immediately.

Pate Brisee

Yield: Enough for a 10″ to 11″ pie or 4 individual pies or tarts.

Measure	Ingredients
1⅓ c	All-purpose flour
4 oz	Butter, cold, cut into 8 pieces
1 each	Egg
⅛ tsp	Salt
1½ tbsp	Water, cold

Directions

1. Cut in All-purpose flour and butter with pastry cutter or 2 knives until the size of peas.

2. Add egg, salt, and water, and mix quickly.

3. Turn out on a floured board, and form a ball; let rest 3 minutes.

4. Roll out dough for tart.

Activity 10.6
Lab—Cuisine of Central America and the Caribbean

Directions

Explore the exotic flavors of the Caribbean and Central America while discovering old and new cooking methods.

Recipe Selection

- Fried Plantains
- *Curtido*
- Jamaican Jerked Pork Chop
- *Gallo Pinto*

Objectives

After completing this lab activity, you should be able to:

- Apply effective *mise en place*
- Demonstrate proper use of equipment and tools
- Follow basic food safety and sanitation guidelines
- Follow basic safety guidelines to avoid causing injury to self or others
- Prepare and serve a variety of Caribbean and Central American dishes

Directions

1. Review the recipe you have been assigned.
2. Perform *mise en place*.
3. Plan for any substitutions or additional ingredients you have been given.
4. Prepare the recipe and present your product.
5. Clean the area.

Fried Plantains

Yield: 2 servings

Measure	Ingredients
5 tbsp	Vegetable oil
1	Plantain, peeled and cut into strips about ¼-in thick
To taste	Salt, kosher
As needed	Sugar, optional
As needed	Cinnamon, optional

Directions

1. Heat the oil in a large skillet.

2. Place the plantain strips in the oil, and fry on both sides, approximately 3½ minutes or until golden.

3. Remove the plantains, and drain on a paper towel-lined plate.

4. Season with Kosher salt alone, Kosher salt and sugar, or Kosher salt and cinnamon.

Curtido

Yield: 4–6 servings

Measure	Ingredients
4 c	Water
½ head	Green cabbage, shredded
1	Carrot, peeled, grated
3	Scallions, minced
½ c	White vinegar
½ c	Water
1	Jalapeño pepper, minced
½ tsp	Salt

Directions

1. In a medium saucepan, bring the 4 cups of water to boil.

2. Place the cabbage and carrot in a large, stainless steel bowl, and pour the boiling water into the bowl until the cabbage and carrots are covered. Set aside for approximately 5 minutes.

3. After 5 minutes, drain the mixture, pressing out as much moisture as possible.

4. Return the cabbage and carrot mixture to the bowl, and add the remaining ingredients. Cover and let sit at room temperature for 2 hours.

5. Place the bowl in the refrigerator, and chill for an additional 2 hours or until just before service.

Jamaican Jerked Pork Chop

Yield: 10 servings

Measure	Ingredients
2	Habañero chilis, stemmed, chopped
8 oz	Scallions, chopped
2 tbsp	Thyme, dried
1 tbsp	Sugar
2 tsp	Salt
1 tsp	Black pepper
1½ tsp	Allspice, ground
1½ tsp	Nutmeg, ground
1 tbsp	Cinnamon, ground
4 fl oz	Olive oil
1 fl oz	Cider vinegar
4 lb	Pork chops, boneless

Directions

1. In a food processor, combine all ingredients (except the pork), and purée.

2. Using gloves, rub the jerk sauce into the pork chops, place into a large covered container, and marinate overnight, in the refrigerator.

3. The next day, grill the jerked pork chops for 7–9 minutes per side. The meat should be tender and cooked through; the internal temperature should be 160°F.

Gallo Pinto

Yield: 6 servings

Measure	Ingredients
1 tbsp	Vegetable oil
1 medium	Onion, chopped
1 small	Red pepper, medium dice
10 sprigs	Cilantro, chopped
4 c	White rice, cooked
1 lb dried or 2 (15.5 oz) cans	Black beans, rinsed, drained
To taste	Worcestershire sauce
½ tsp	Salt

Directions

1. In a large skillet heat the oil, and sauté the onion, pepper, and cilantro until tender.

2. Add the rice and beans, and stir until all ingredients are mixed.

3. Season with Worcestershire sauce and salt.

4. Continue to cook, stirring frequently, until rice begins to brown lightly.

5. Serve with eggs or a flour tortilla.

Activity 10.7
Editorial—Stevia: Friend or Foe?

Directions

Write an editorial for or against FDA approval of stevia. Find statistics about the advantages or disadvantages of using this plant as a dietary sweetener. Research the topic using trusted Internet sources, culinary magazines, health-food magazines, and cookbooks. Be sure to document your sources and include at least three different sources to support your point of view.

Take your notes in the space below. Use a separate sheet of paper or your computer to create your editorial.

_____

_____

_____

_____

_____

_____

_____

_____

_____

_____

_____

_____

_____

_____

_____

_____

_____

_____

_____

_____

_____

_____

_____

Activity 10.8
Create a Dinner from Central or South America

Directions

You have been asked by a local restaurant to help with a new promotion that they are going to run during the summer featuring dinners from around the world. The chef would like you to create a three-course dinner featuring the food of Central or South America. Your dinner should include an appetizer (this could also be a salad or soup), an entrée (include a starch and vegetable), and a dessert. The chef would also like recipes for each item that can be shared with the guests.

Describe each dish and the cooking technique used on one page. Then, create an additional page for each menu item that identifies the nutritional information and cost of each ingredient.

Use other cookbooks, online recipe sites, and sites about each country to gather information about the food and culture of the country selected.

Take your notes in the space below. Use a separate sheet of paper or your computer to create your menu.

_____

_____

_____

_____

_____

_____

_____

_____

_____

_____

_____

_____

_____

_____

_____

_____

_____

_____

Activity 10.9
Lab— Food of South America

Directions

South American cuisine is very similar to many styles of North American cuisine, using large amounts of beef and potatoes. Explore the similarities of the cultures as you experience some traditional South American dishes.

Recipe Selection

- Feijoada
- Ceviche of Scallops
- Brazilian Style Flan (*Pudim de Leite Condensada*)

Objectives

After completing this lab activity, you should be able to:

- Apply effective *mise en place*
- Demonstrate proper use of equipment and tools
- Follow basic food safety and sanitation guidelines
- Follow basic safety guidelines to avoid causing injury to self or others
- Prepare and serve a variety of South American dishes

Directions

1. Review the recipe you have been assigned.
2. Perform *mise en place.*
3. Plan for any substitutions or additional ingredients you have been given.
4. Prepare and present the recipe.
5. Clean the area.

Feijoada

Yield: 8–10 servings

Measure	Ingredients
2 (15 ½ oz) cans	Black beans, rinsed and drained
1 lb	Ham hocks, smoked
1 lb	Mexican sausage (or other spicy smoked sausage)
½ lb	Canadian bacon
½ lb	Pork, smoked
3–4 strips	Bacon, smoked, slab
½ lb	Lean pork, cut into ½″ cubes
½ lb	Lean beef, cut into ½″ cubes
1 large	Onion, chopped
4 cloves	Garlic, minced
2 tbsp	Olive oil
1 tbsp	Vinegar, white
1 tsp	Hot pepper, minced
To taste	Salt
To taste	Pepper
To taste	Hot sauce

Directions

1. In a large pot, heat the black beans until tender.

2. In a large covered pot, add the ham hocks, sausage, bacon, and smoked pork. Cover with water and bring to a boil. Drain the pot, add more water, and boil a second time. Repeat once more until the meats are tender, and the fat is removed.

3. In a large skillet, sauté the onions and garlic with the vegetable oil for 2–3 minutes, until tender. Stir in the beef and pork cubes, and sauté an additional 3–4 minutes.

4. In a small frying pan, add olive oil, garlic, vinegar, and hot pepper. Stir over medium heat for 2–3 minutes, and then add the to frying pan with the cubed beef and pork.

5. Let the mixture simmer for 10 minutes, and then add to the beans, and cook for another hour or until tender.

Ceviche of Scallops

Yield: 10 servings

Measure	Ingredients
1 lb, 4 oz	Sea scallops*, muscle removed, thinly sliced
10 oz	Tomato concassé
6 fl oz	Lemon or lime juice
3 oz	Red onion rings, thinly sliced
2 oz	Scallions, bias cut
2 fl oz	Olive oil
½ oz	Jalapeno peppers, fine dice
1 tsp	Garlic clove, mashed to paste
1.2 oz	Cilantro, chopped
10 fl oz	Guacamole

* Note: A less expensive fish can be used in place of scallops; choose a firm fleshed fish.

Directions

1. Combine all the ingredients. Marinate the scallops (or seafood) for a minimum of 4 hours and up to 12 hours before service.

2. Serve the ceviche cold, with guacamole, on chilled plates.

Note:

Concassé the tomatoes by removing the hard stem section and making a small X with a knife on the bottom. Boil the tomatoes about 1 minute, and then remove with a slotted spoon or tongs. Place immediately in ice water to cool. After about 1 minute you will be able to peel the skin easily. Next, cut the tomatoes across, and remove the seeds with your fingers. After removing the seeds, coarsely chop the tomatoes.

Brazilian Style Flan *(Pudim de Leite Condensada)*

Yield: 8 Servings

Measure	Ingredients
1 cup	Sugar
4	Eggs, separated
1 (14 oz) can	Sweetened condensed milk
¾ cup plus 2 Tbsp	Milk

Directions

1. Preheat oven to 350°F.

2. In a medium saucepan, over low heat, melt the sugar, stirring constantly.

3. After approximately 10 minutes, the sugar will turn to a golden-brown syrup. Immediately pour the syrup into a round baking dish. Swirl the syrup so all sides of the baking dish are coated. Set aside.

4. In a blender, place the egg yolks, and blend on medium for 5 minutes, and then add the condensed milk, ¾ cup plus 2 tablespoons of milk, and egg whites. Continue to blend until all ingredients are combined.

5. Pour egg mixture into baking dish, and cover with aluminum foil.

6. Line a roasting pan with a damp kitchen towel. Place the baking dish on the towel, inside the roasting pan. Place the roasting pan on the oven rack.

7. Fill the roasting pan half-way with boiling water; do not let water get into the baking dish.

8. Bake for approximately 45-50 minutes, until a knife inserted 1″ from the edge of the baking dish comes out clean.

9. The center of the flan will still be soft.

10. Refrigerate flan before unmolding onto plate.

Activity 10.10
Brochure—A South American Food Adventure

Directions

You have been hired by a local travel agency to create a travel brochure promoting their newest two-week travel adventure—an exploration of South American culture and cuisines.

Design a trifold brochure that will encourage travelers to go to South America on a gourmet vacation. In the brochure be sure to use pictures and descriptive text to highlight the following elements of the tour:

- Food of two or three countries
- Geography
- Natural attractions
- Man-made attractions
- Brief history of each country

Take your notes in the space below. Use a separate sheet of paper or your computer to create your brochure.

_____
_____
_____
_____
_____
_____
_____
_____
_____
_____
_____
_____
_____
_____
_____
_____
_____
_____

Chapter **11**

Activity 11.1
Test Your Knowledge of Global Cuisines—Europe, the Mediterranean, the Middle East, and Asia IQ

Directions

Mark each of the following statements related to global cuisine as either true (T) or false (F). Rewrite the false statements to make them true.

Part 1—Europe

_____ 1. A brigade is a group of workers assigned a specific set of tasks in the kitchen.

_____

_____

_____ 2. Haute cuisine is characterized by simple flavors and lighter dishes.

_____

_____

_____ 3. Italian food is often associated with the cuisine of poverty, featuring simple and filling foods.

_____

_____

_____ 4. There are few regional differences in Italian cuisine, the largest being the types of cheese used in pasta dishes.

_____

_____

_____ 5. *Pimientos del piquillo* are very hot peppers that are commonly used in several Spanish dishes.

_____

_____

_____ 6. The most expensive spice in the world is saffron and comes from the saffron crocus flower.

_____

_____

Part 2—The Mediterranean

_____ 1. The Arabs, who occupied Morocco during the seventh century, played a major role in determining the cuisine of the Mediterranean by introducing new spices and the concept of combining sweet and sour tastes.

_____

_____

_____ 2. *Tagine* can refer to either a meat stew cooked for a long time and made from lamb, fish, or game, or the earthenware cooking dish used to make the stew.

_____

_____

_____ 3. Baklava is a traditional dish made from lamb and eggplant, and then covered with a béchamel sauce.

_____

_____

_____ 4. Phyllo, *warqa*, and *maloufa* are different names for the same dough product.

_____

_____

_____ 5. *Chermoula* is a classic Tunisian dish that is a mixture of goat, feta cheese, saffron, and ginger served over spicy couscous.

_____

_____

_____ 6. There are many similarities between French and Tunisian food—for example, *chakchouka*, which is a type of ratatouille.

_____

_____

Part 3—The Middle East

_____ 1. Egypt is located in the Fertile Crescent of the Nile Valley, but must still import 60 percent of its food because of the vast desserts surrounding most of the country.

_____

_____

_____ 2. *Baba ghanoush* is an Egyptian street food very similar to the Greek gyro.

_____

_____

_____ 3. Iranian culture and cuisine were greatly influenced by its location on the Silk Road, a trade conduit between China and Italy.

_____

_____

_____ 4. Iranian desserts tend to be more savory then sweet, and one dessert is even made from minced lamb or chicken.

_____

_____

_____ 5. A typical Saudi Arabian meal consists of several very small courses, served hot or cold, followed with a sweet dessert.

_____

_____

_____ 6. In Saudi Arabia, dairy products are commonly made from cow's milk and include yogurt and ice cream.

_____

_____

Part 4—Asia

_____ 1. Chinese cuisine follows the yin and yang principles of the Tao, believing all foods have a specific purpose.

_____

_____

_____ 2. The three most popular styles of Chinese cooking are Mandarin, Szechwan-Hunan, and Cantonese.

_____

_____

_____ 3. _Cha kalseki_ is a Japanese ceremony and cuisine that developed around sushi.

_____

_____

_____ 4. Japanese cuisine is based on hot, spicy sauces and powders.

_____

_____

_____ 5. Curry is both the name of a spice and a type of dish served in many Indian restaurants.

_____

_____

_____ 6. An unusual cooking method found in India is called _tarka_, which is the technique of scattering whole or ground dried spices into hot oil until they pop and flavor the oil.

_____

_____

Activity 11.2
Crossword Puzzle—Global Cuisines 2

Directions

Complete the following statements, and then use the answers to complete the crossword puzzle.

ACROSS

3. This Indian spice, _____, is made from several strong tasting spices including black cardamom, black pepper, and clove.

6. Egyptian _____ is made from shredded meat served on a pita and is very similar to a gyro.

7. A double boiler used to cook couscous is called a _____.

8. The countries of North Africa are known as _____.

10. This seasoning made from dried Ormani lime is called _____ and is a popular Saudia Arabian spice.

11. Europeans refused to eat _____ for centuries, fearing that they were poisonous.

13. _____ oranges were introduced to Spain by the Arabs.

16. _____ were introduced to Italy by Greek invaders in 415 BC.

17. _____ is made from soybeans and makes a nearly nutritionally perfect meal when paired with rice.

20. _____ cuisine is found in the northern region of China and includes bird's nest soup and Peking duck.

21. _____ is known as the culinary center of France.

22. One of many olives that come from Greece is the _____.

DOWN

1. The _____ introduced farming to the French around 1500 BCE.

2. The world's most expensive spice is _____, which requires over 50,000 crocus flowers to make one pound of spice.

3. This famous cheese _____ _____ _____ is made from the milk of water buffaloes.

4. The Fertile _____ refers to the Nile Valley.

5. People who travel solely to experience the food and drink from a particular area are referred to as _____ .

7. Normandy is known not only for the role it played in WWII but also for this cheese called _____ .

9. _____ sauce is made from toasted and ground nuts, toasted bread, garlic, and fresh herbs.

12. A group of workers assigned a specific set of tasks in the traditional French kitchen is known as a _____ .

14. A rich delicacy made from sheets of *warqa*, almonds, and pastry cream is known as _____ .

15. _____ is a traditional Greek casserole made from lamb and eggplant.

18. The _____ road is a well-known trading route of ancient Chinese civilization.

19. _____ means both cooked rice and meal in Japanese.

20. The _____ invaded France in 718 AD and brought new ingredients with them, such as caraway and cinnamon.

Activity 11.3
Lab—European Cuisine

Directions

Many Americans have European roots, and most people are familiar with variations of many European dishes. Some items seem overwhelming or difficult to prepare until you actually make them.

Recipe Selection

- Bubble and Squeak (English fried potatoes and cabbage)
- Crêpes Suzette (French thin pancakes with orange sauce)
- Kartoffelsalat (German potato salad)
- Dolmades (Greek stuffed grape leaves)
- Gazpacho (Spanish cold-tomato soup)

Objectives

After completing this lab activity, you should be able to:

- Apply effective *mise en place*
- Demonstrate proper use of equipment and tools
- Follow basic food safety and sanitation guidelines
- Follow basic safety guidelines to avoid causing injury to self or others
- Prepare and be familiar with a variety of European dishes

Directions

1. Review the recipe you have been assigned.
2. Perform *mise en place.*
3. Plan for any substitutions or additional ingredients you have been given.
4. Prepare the recipe.
5. Clean the area.

Bubble and Squeak

Yield: 4–6 servings

Measure	Ingredients
3	Potatoes
½ head	Cabbage
To taste	Salt
To taste	Pepper
1 small	Onion, diced
3 tbsp	Oil (or butter)

Directions

1. Peel potatoes, and then cut into small cubes. Cook in boiling water until soft.

2. Drain potatoes, and mash them so they are still lumpy.

3. Cook the cabbage in boiling water or steam until soft, about 15 minutes.

4. Cut the cabbage up into small pieces, about 2″ in size.

5. Mix the potatoes and cabbage together in a bowl, and season with salt and pepper.

6. Peel and dice the onion.

7. Heat the oil in a heavy skillet over medium high heat. Sauté the onion until translucent.

8. Stir in the potato-cabbage mixture, and press down into the skillet.

9. Reduce the heat to medium and cook, undisturbed, until the bottom is brown, approximately 10 minutes.

10. Flip the potato mixture and brown the other side.

11. This dish may be served hot or cold, depending on the chef's preference.

Note:

Served cold, this is an excellent side dish for sandwiches. When served hot, it is an excellent breakfast dish and can be made with leftovers.

This dish can also be made with meat, but is traditionally made with potatoes and cabbage.

Crêpes Suzette

Yield: 15

Measure	Ingredients
Crêpes	
¾ c	Flour
½ c	Milk
½ c	Water
2 each	Eggs
Pinch	Salt
2 tbsp	Butter, melted, or non-stick spray
Sauce for Crêpes	
8 oz	Butter, room temperature
1 tbsp	Orange zest
⅔ cup	Orange juice
½ cup	Sugar

Directions

1. Combine the flour, milk, water, eggs, and salt, and whisk until smooth. Chill for at least 30 minutes.

2. Melt a little butter in a small- or medium-sized non-stick skillet over medium heat.

3. Using a 1 ounce ladle or measuring cup, pour about 2 tablespoons of the crêpe batter onto the heated pan, and swirl the pan so the batter just coats the bottom.

4. Cook until the crêpe appears dry and has started to brown on the bottom. This will only be about 1 minute.

5. Flip the crêpe onto parchment paper, then cover with another piece of parchment, and continue to layer the crêpes.

6. Repeat with the remaining batter, spraying the pan only as needed so the crêpes do not stick.

Note:

The crêpes can be made ahead of time and refrigerated if desired.

Orange Sauce

1. Heat the butter and orange zest in a skillet or chafing dish over medium heat.

2. Add the orange juice and sugar, and whisk until the sugar is completely dissolved and the sauce is bubbling, 2–3 minutes.

3. Dip a crêpe into the orange sauce with tongs, turning to cover both sides with the orange sauce. Fold the crêpe in half, and then half again, so you end up with a shape that looks like a quarter of a pie.

4. Repeat with the remaining crêpes, and pour any remaining sauce over the crêpes.

5. Serve immediately.

Kartoffelsalat

Yield: 4–6 servings

Measure	Ingredients
2 lb	Potatoes
4 slices	Bacon
4 tsp	Onion, diced
⅓ c	Vinegar
¼ c	Sugar
1 tsp	Dry mustard (or 1 tbsp prepared mustard)
1 tsp	Salt
¼ tsp	Black pepper, ground
¼ tsp	Dill
1 tsp	Parsley, chopped

Directions

1. Wash and peel the potatoes; dice into about 2″ size.
2. Add the potatoes to a large pot, and cover with cold water.
3. Bring the water to a boil, and then reduce to a simmer.
4. Cook potatoes until a fork can enter the potato easily.
5. Drain the potatoes, and let steam dry. (Do not refrigerate or pat dry.)
6. Cook bacon until crispy, and then drain and crumble.
7. Peel and dice 4 teaspoons of onion.
8. In a large bowl, whisk the onion, vinegar, sugar, mustard, salt, pepper, and dill. Add the bacon to the mixture.
9. Place the still-warm potatoes into the bowl, and stir. The potatoes might break up a little, but this is natural and is the look of the dish.
10. Garnish with parsley.

Dolmades

Yield: 50 servings

Measure	Ingredients
½	Onion, chopped
2 tbsp	Oil
½ lb	Lamb, ground
½ c	Rice, uncooked
½ tsp	Salt
⅓ tsp	Allspice
1 tbsp	Parsley
2 tbsp	Butter, melted butter
1	Jar of grape leaves

Directions

1. Sauté onions in oil until translucent.

2. Add ground lamb, rice, salt, allspice, chopped parsley, and melted butter.

3. Mix thoroughly.

4. Drain liquid from the grape leaves, and then rinse in hot water.

5. Place the grape leaves shiny-side down, and fill with 1 tablespoon of mixture.

6. Fold the leaf from the stem down over the sides as an envelope. (Rolls must be tight.)

7. Lay the stuffed leaves in the bottom of a pan, wedging them close together.

8. Pour enough water to cover the stuffed leaves, and cook until the leaves are tender, about 1½ hours.

Gazpacho

Yield: 4 servings

Measure	Ingredients
1½–2 lbs	Tomatoes
1	Cucumber
1	Bell pepper, green or red
1	Red onion
3	Garlic cloves
2 tbsp	Lime juice, fresh
¾ c	Water or tomato juice
¼ c	Red wine vinegar
¼ c	Parsley, fresh, chopped
¼ c	Olive oil, extra virgin
To taste	Salt
To taste	Pepper
Dash	Hot sauce
½–1 c	Garlic croutons (recipe follows)
As needed	Olive oil

Directions

1. Concassé the tomatoes.

2. Peel and seed the cucumber by cutting in half long ways. Remove the seeds with a parisienne scoop or teaspoon.

3. Core and seed bell pepper.

4. Peel and dice the red onion.

5. Take 3 garlic cloves, and mince them.

6. Take one half of the tomatoes, chopped cucumber, bell pepper, and red onion, and combine with all of the garlic, lime juice, water or tomato juice, and red wine vinegar, and purée until smooth. Transfer the purée into a container.

7. Add the remaining tomatoes, chopped cucumber, bell pepper, and red onion into the blender with the ¼ cup parsley and ¼ cup olive oil, and pulse to a chunky state.

8. Combine the purée and the chunky vegetable mix.

9. Refrigerate until well chilled.

10. Season before serving with salt, pepper, and Tabasco.

11. Serve in a chilled bowl garnished with garlic croutons or diced cucumber and a drizzle of olive oil.

Note: Concassé the tomatoes by removing the hard stem section and making a small X with a knife on the bottom. Boil the tomatoes about 1 minute, and then remove with a slotted spoon or tongs. Place immediately in ice water to cool. After about 1 minute you will be able to peel the skin easily. Next, cut the tomatoes across, and remove the seeds with your fingers. After removing the seeds, coarsely chop the tomatoes.

Garlic Croutons

Measure	Ingredients
2	Garlic cloves
1 tbsp	Olive oil
1 c	Bread cubes, day-old

Directions

1. Mince the garlic.

2. Heat the oil in a skillet; add garlic.

3. Cook the minced garlic.

4. Add the bread cubes, and cook until brown.

Note:

You may also coat the bread cubes in the garlic and olive oil, spread on a sheet pan, and cook in a 350°F oven for about 15 minutes.

Activity 11.4
Presentation—Modern Chefs and Their Impact on the Culinary Scene

Directions

Food trends develop and change over time, and many chefs have been credited with introducing new foods or new cooking techniques to diners around the world. Choose from one of the chefs suggested below, and research that chef and the impact that he or she has had on contemporary food and cooking. Present your research to the class in the form of a PowerPoint, Web page, or brochure. Be sure to include the following information:

- Where was he or she was born? (Include a map if possible.)

- How did he or she get started cooking?

- Did geography play a role in the type of food this chef is known for?

- Where is he or she currently cooking? (Or, if deceased, where did he or she cook?)

- What is he or she best known for in the culinary world?

- What is his or her signature dish? (Include the recipe if possible.)

Select a chef from the following list or another modern chef that is approved by your instructor.

Antonio Carluccio	Lucas Ndlovu
Julia Child	Ferran Adria Acosta
Pierre Gagnaire	Gordon Ramsay
Alain Ducasse	Mario Batali
Emeril Lagasse	Jamie Oliver
Fernand Point	Sanjeev Kapoor
Alice Waters	Rachel Ray

Take your notes in the space below. Use a separate sheet of paper, poster board, or your computer to create your presentation.

_____

_____

_____

_____

_____

_____

_____

Activity 11.5
Lab—Mediterranean Cuisine

Directions

The line that defines the Mediterranean countries from European countries is not clearly defined, and many of the tastes and flavors travel between the countries. Explore some of the unique tastes of this area.

Recipe Selection

- Horiatiki Salata (Greek salad)
- Moroccan Couscous with Brunoise Peppers
- Baklava (Turkish pastry)
- Mediterranean Tomato Sauce

Objectives

After completing this lab activity, you should be able to:

- Apply effective *mise en place*
- Demonstrate proper use of equipment and tools
- Follow basic food safety and sanitation guidelines
- Follow basic safety guidelines to avoid causing injury to self or others
- Prepare and serve a variety of Mediterranean dishes

Directions

1. Review the recipe you have been assigned.
2. Perform *mise en place.*
3. Plan for any substitutions or additional ingredients you have been given.
4. Prepare the recipe.
5. Clean the area.

Horiatiki Salata

Yield: 4 salads

Measure	Ingredients
Dressing for Salad	
½ cup	Olive oil
¼ cup	Red wine vinegar
1 clove	Garlic, minced
1 tbsp	Oregano, fresh, chopped (or 1 tsp dried)
To taste	Salt
To taste	Pepper
Salad	
½ head	Romaine lettuce
3	Tomatoes, seeded and diced
½	Cucumber, peeled, seeded, cubed
½	Red onion, halved, thinly sliced
½ c	Kalamata olives
½ lb	Feta cheese

Directions
Dressing

1. Combine the olive oil, red wine vinegar, minced garlic, and oregano, and whisk with a wire whisk.

2. Add salt and pepper to taste.

3. Refrigerate until service with the salad.

Salad

1. Wash the romaine lettuce by removing the leaves and running under cold water. Dry well so the oil will adhere to the leaves. This can be done with a salad spinner, by gently shaking the leaves, or by using paper towels.

2. Chop the lettuce into bite-sized pieces.

3. Concassé the tomatoes.

4. Peel the cucumber, or use a channel knife to remove some of the skin.

5. Cut the cucumber in half lengthwise, and remove the center section of seeds with a small parisienne scoop.

6. Chop one half of the cucumber into bite-sized pieces.

7. Slice the red onion very thinly.

8. Combine the lettuce, tomatoes, cucumbers, red onion slices, and Kalamata olives.

9. The feta cheese is served as a whole wedge on each plate in Greece; in the United States, the feta cheese is normally crumbled. This is the chef's choice.

10. Serve the salad with the dressing.

Note:

Concassé the tomatoes by removing the hard stem section and making a small X with a knife on the bottom. Boil the tomatoes about 1 minute, and then remove with a slotted spoon or tongs. Place immediately in ice water to cool. After about 1 minute you will be able to peel the skin easily. Next, cut the tomatoes across, and remove the seeds with your fingers. After removing the seeds, coarsely chop the tomatoes.

This salad should be ⅓ lettuce and ⅔ tomatoes. You will have to judge by the size of your romaine lettuce and the size of your tomatoes if you need to cut back on lettuce or add tomato.

Moroccan Couscous with Brunoise Peppers

Yield: 4 servings

Measure	Ingredients
¾ cup	Heavy cream
2 tsp	Salt
½ tsp	Cinnamon
¼ tsp	Nutmeg
¼ tsp	Ginger
¾ cup	Couscous
¾ cup	Parmesan cheese, grated
¼ each	Green pepper
¼ each	Red pepper
¼ each	Yellow pepper
2 tsp	Vegetable oil

Directions

1. Heat the heavy cream and water, adding 2 teaspoon of salt.

2. Combine the cinnamon, nutmeg, and ginger.

3. When the cream comes to a simmer, add the couscous and the spices, and stir well until fully incorporated.

4. Remove couscous from the heat, and add cheese.

5. Cover the couscous, and let rest for 5 minutes.

6. Season to taste with salt.

7. Clean, core, and remove seeds from the peppers.

8. Cut each pepper brunoise.

9. Sauté lightly in oil.

10. Combine peppers with couscous and serve.

Variation

This dish can be made with different flavors of couscous.

Baklava

Yield: 24 pieces

Measure	Ingredients
Baklava	
1 c	Butter
1½ lb	Nuts, chopped (pistachios, walnuts, pecans, etc.)
½ c	Sugar
½ tsp	Cinnamon
⅛ tsp	Ground cloves
1 tsp	Vanilla extract
1 pkg	Phyllo dough
Syrup	
2 c	Sugar
2 c	Water
1 c	Honey
2 tbsp	Lemon juice, fresh or extract

Directions

1. Preheat oven to 350°F.

2. Melt the butter.

3. Chop the nuts, and then combine nuts, sugar, cinnamon, ground cloves, and vanilla.

4. Lightly coat a half sheet pan (13″ × 18″).

5. Unroll the phyllo dough. Cover with plastic wrap and a barely-damp cloth to keep the dough from drying out. (If it is too wet, it will ruin the dough.)

6. Cut the dough in half to fit the pan. Place 2 sheets of dough in the bottom of the pan, and brush with the melted butter.

7. Add another sheet and brush with butter, continuing until you have about 8 sheets.

8. Spread about ⅓ of the nut mixture on the phyllo dough, and then cover with a sheet of dough. Brush butter on the dough, and continue to layer the dough until you have about 4 sheets of dough.

9. Brush with butter, and then spread ⅓ of the nut mixture on the dough.

10. Cover with phyllo dough layered with butter until you have 4 sheets.

11. Repeat with the remaining ⅓ of the nut mixture, and top with 8 sheets of dough layered with brushed butter.

12. Brush the top layer.

13. Cut into diamonds or squares, about 2″ × 2″, using a sharp knife.

14. Bake in preheated oven for 45 minutes to 1 hour, or until golden brown.

15. While baklava is cooking, make the syrup for the dish.

Directions for Syrup

1. Combine sugar, water, honey, and lemon juice in a sauce pan.

2. Bring mixture to a full boil, and then turn down the heat and simmer about 10 minutes.

3. Cool at room temperature.

4. When baklava is taken from the oven, cut over the same lines with a sharp knife.

5. Spoon the cooled syrup over the baklava, and then allow to cool so it can be removed from the pan easily.

Note:

The recipe for baklava spread from the Mediterranean and the Middle East to the Near East, Armenia, and Turkey. Phyllo dough is named after the Greek word for "leaf," being "as thin as a leaf." The thickness (or for that matter, the thinness) of phyllo gives baklava its delicious, crispy taste.

Mediterranean Tomato Sauce

Yield: 6 servings

Measure	Ingredients
4 lb	Tomatoes
3	Shallots
2	Garlic cloves
1	Fennel, small
½ tbsp	Olive oil, extra virgin
½ tsp	Salt
¼ tsp	Pepper, freshly ground
1 bunch	Parsley

Directions

1. Concassé the tomatoes.

2. Chop shallots finely.

3. Mince garlic cloves.

4. Dice fennel.

5. In a large skillet, heat the extra virgin olive oil

6. Add tomatoes, shallot, garlic, and fennel, and cook for about 5 minutes until tomatoes soften and the excess liquid has evaporated. Season with salt and fresh-ground pepper.

7. Chop ½ the parsley finely, reserving other half for garnish, if desired.

8. Stir in parsley.

Note:

Concassé the tomatoes by removing the hard stem section and making a small X with a knife on the bottom. Boil the tomatoes about 1 minute, and then remove with a slotted spoon or tongs. Place immediately in ice water to cool. After about 1 minute you will be able to peel the skin easily. Next, cut the tomatoes across, and remove the seeds with your fingers. After removing the seeds, coarsely chop the tomatoes.

This tomato sauce is the basis for many recipes. The sauce can be used over pasta for a quick and delicious meal. It is often used in the bottom of a pan with either chicken or a solid fish and cooked until the meat is done. It can also be served over fish or chicken as a sauce.

Activity 11.6
News Article—The Mediterranean Diet

Directions

The owner of the Easy Street Café is considering opening a new restaurant that will have a more European flair. She has hired you to write a 500-word article on the health benefits of the Mediterranean diet. She would like your article to include at least four different recipe suggestions that can be used as possible specials in the restaurant. The article should focus on the health benefits, how the Mediterranean diet compares to the more-typical American diet, and two to three tips for eating healthy while dining out.

Take your notes in the space below. Use a separate sheet of paper, or your computer to create your article.

_____

_____

_____

_____

_____

_____

_____

_____

_____

_____

_____

_____

_____

_____

_____

_____

_____

_____

_____

_____

_____

Activity 11.7
Lab—Middle Eastern Cuisine

Directions

Middle Eastern cuisine is unique in its use of flavors, such as saffron and rose water. Many of the dishes demonstrate a balance of sweet and sour within the same dish. Eggplant is another ingredient found in many of these dishes. Working with eggplant forms a good base.

Recipe Selection

- *Baba Ghanoush*
- Hummus
- Tabbouleh
- Lamb Kebabs

Objectives

After completing this lab activity, you should be able to:

- Apply effective *mise en place*
- Demonstrate proper use of equipment and tools
- Follow basic food safety and sanitation guidelines
- Follow basic safety guidelines to avoid causing injury to self or others
- Prepare and serve a variety of Middle Eastern dishes

Directions

1. Review the recipe you have been assigned.
2. Perform *mise en place.*
3. Plan for any substitutions or additional ingredients you have been given.
4. Prepare the recipe.
5. Clean the area.

Baba Ghanoush

Yield: 4 servings

Measure	Ingredients
1	Eggplant (approximately 1 lb)
2 cloves	Garlic
To taste	Salt
1 oz	Tahini paste
2 oz	Lemon juice
1 oz	Olive oil
1 tsp	Cumin
1 oz	Kalamata olives, chopped
1 tbsp	Parsley, flat leaf, chopped

Directions

1. Preheat oven to 350°F.

2. Prick eggplant on all sides, multiple times. Place on a sheet pan, and bake for 20 minutes or until soft.

3. While the eggplant is baking, mince garlic. Add salt to minced garlic, and continue to mash it into a paste with the tip of a French knife.

4. Cool eggplant, and remove skin. Roughly chop the eggplant flesh.

5. In a food processor, combine the eggplant flesh, garlic paste, tahini paste, lemon juice, olive oil, and cumin. Blend until smooth.

6. Place finished product in a bowl and garnish with chopped olives and parsley.

Note:

This may be served with pita chips, crudités, and pita bread.

Hummus

Yield: 16 ounces

Measure	Ingredients
4 cloves	Garlic, roasted
½ lb	Chick peas, cooked
4 oz	Tahini paste
4 cloves	Garlic, roasted
1	Lemon juice
1 oz	Olive oil
To taste	Salt

Directions

1. Roast garlic by preheating oven to 400°F.

2. Peel away outer paper-like layers. Cut off about ¼″ to ½″ off the top of each clove of garlic

3. Place the garlic head on a piece of foil, and drizzle 2 teaspoons of olive oil over it. Use your fingers to make sure the garlic is well coated; use more oil if necessary. Wrap in the foil, and bake for 30 minutes or until the gloves are soft.

4. Allow garlic to cool, and then use your fingers or a fork to squeeze the cloves out of their skins.

5. Combine the garlic, chick peas, tahini paste, and lemon juice in a food processor.

6. Process until smooth.

7. Season with salt.

Variations

Try adding one of the following ingredients to create a new flavor profile:

- 2 tablespoons parsley, chopped
- ¼ cup roasted red pepper, chopped
- ¼ cup caramelized onions, chopped

Tabouleh Salad

Yield: 4 servings

Measure	Ingredients
2 c	Water
1 c	Bulgur wheat
1	Lemon, juice of
2 oz	Olive oil
2 bunches	Parsley, chopped, stems removed
2	Tomato concassé
1	White onion, medium, small dice

Directions

1. In a saucepan, bring 2 cups of water to a boil.

2. Add bulgur wheat, reduce to a simmer, and cook until water is absorbed.

3. Remove cooked bulgur wheat from the pan; spread it out onto a sheet pan, and chill in the cooler.

4. Once the bulgur wheat is chilled, toss it together with the lemon juice, olive oil, chopped parsley, tomato, and diced white onion in a large bowl.

5. Serve cold with pita wedges or as a side salad.

Note:

Concassé the tomatoes by removing the hard stem section and making a small X with a knife on the bottom. Boil the tomatoes about 1 minute, and then remove with a slotted spoon or tongs. Place immediately in ice water to cool. After about 1 minute you will be able to peel the skin easily. Next, cut the tomatoes across, and remove the seeds with your fingers. After removing the seeds, coarsely chop the tomatoes.

Lamb Shish Kebab

Yield: 4 servings

Measure	Ingredients
4 oz	Olive oil
2 oz	Lemon juice
2 tbsp	Garlic, minced
¼ tsp	Salt
¼ tsp	Black pepper, ground
¼ tsp	Greek oregano
½ tsp	Cumin
2	Bay leaves
1 lb	Leg of lamb, boneless, trimmed, cut into ½″ pieces
1	Yellow onion, cut into ½″ pieces
1	Green bell pepper, cut into ½″ pieces
8	Button mushrooms, whole
8	Cherry tomatoes
8	Wooden skewers, soaked in water to prevent burning

Directions

1. In a large bowl, combine olive oil, lemon juice, garlic, salt, pepper, oregano, cumin, and bay leaves.
2. Add the lamb and marinade for a minimum of 30 minutes.
3. Begin skewering the lamb and vegetables, alternating between lamb, yellow onion, green pepper, mushroom, and cherry tomato.
4. Grill to the desired doneness.

Note:

As a general rule it will take about 1½–2 minutes per side (there are 4 sides on a kebab), or a total cooking time of just under 8 minutes. All equipment works differently, so use a meat thermometer to check for doneness at about 150°F–165°F. Be careful not to overcook.

Activity 11.8
Flavor Chart—Middle Eastern Cuisine

Directions

You will be participating in a taste test to identify different flavors commonly found in Middle Eastern cooking. As you taste each flavor, record your impressions on the chart provided. Compare how these spices are used in Middle Eastern cuisine and in western countries.

Flavor Chart

Spice Name	Smell	Color	Taste	Texture

Activity 11.9
Lab—Asian Cuisine

Directions

The cuisines of Asia are known around the world, and many of the more popular dishes are readily available in restaurants around the country. Explore the variety of tastes and textures found in these foods.

Recipe Selection

- Tandoori Chicken
- Vegetable Curry
- Vegetable Tempura
- Hot and Sour Soup

Objectives

After completing this lab activity, you should be able to:

- Apply effective *mise en place*
- Demonstrate proper use of equipment and tools
- Follow basic food safety and sanitation guidelines
- Follow basic safety guidelines to avoid causing injury to self or others
- Prepare and serve a variety of Asian dishes

Directions

1. Review the recipe you have been assigned.
2. Perform *mise en place.*
3. Plan for any substitutions or additional ingredients you have been given.
4. Prepare and present the recipe.
5. Clean the area.

Tandoori Chicken

Yield: 10 servings

Measure	Ingredients
8 oz	Yogurt, nonfat
1 fl oz	Water
2 oz	Ginger, minced
1 tbsp	Cumin, ground
1 tbsp	Cardamom, ground
1 tbsp	Coriander, ground
½ tsp	Saffron
½ tsp	Cayenne, ground
4 cloves	Garlic, minced
10	Chicken breasts

Directions

1. Combine the yogurt, water, and seasonings in a large bowl.

2. Place the chicken breasts in the yogurt mixture, and marinate, in the refrigerator, for 12 hours.

3. Remove the chicken from the marinade, and allow any excess to drain away. Place the chicken presentation side down on the grill.

4. Grill over medium high heat for 3 minutes undisturbed. Turn the chicken over, and complete cooking until done, about 3 or 4 more minutes or until an internal temperature of 170°F is reached.

Vegetable Curry

Yield: 4–6 servings

Measure	Ingredients
1 tbsp	Olive oil
1	Onion, medium, chopped
2 cloves	Garlic, crushed
2½ tbsp	Curry powder (see recipe below)
2 tbsp	Tomato paste
1 can (14.5 oz)	Tomatoes, diced
1½ c	Vegetable broth
2 c	Vegetables, fresh, mixed, chopped (carrots, broccoli, cauliflower, beans, etc.)
To taste	Salt
To taste	Pepper
2 tbsp	Cilantro, fresh, chopped

Directions

1. In a large saucepan, heat oil and sauté onion and garlic until golden. Stir in curry and tomato paste, and cook 2–3 minutes.

2. Stir in tomatoes, broth, and carrots. Cook for approximately 10 minutes, and then add cauliflower and broccoli. Cook for an additional 10 minutes, and then stir in the beans.

3. Continue cooking until vegetables are well done and not crunchy.

4. Garnish with cilantro.

Curry Powder

Measure	Ingredients
⅛ c	Turmeric powder
3 tsp	Whole cardamom seeds
3 tsp	Whole cumin seeds
3 tsp	Whole coriander seeds
¼ tsp	Cinnamon powder
½ tsp	Cayenne pepper

Directions

1. Lightly toast the cardamom, coriander, and cumin seeds.
2. Grind toasted seeds in a coffee grinder.
3. Place in a jar and add remaining spices.
4. Shake until thoroughly mixed.

Vegetable Tempura

Yield: 2–4 servings

Measure	Ingredients
1 c	Vegetable oil
1 c	All-purpose flour
½ c	Corn flour
¼ c	Ice water
1 large	Zucchini, cut in 3″ strips
1 large	Carrot, cut in rounds
1 medium	Sweet potato, julienne
1 small head	Broccoli, cut in bite-sized pieces
4 oz	Button mushrooms, washed and dried

Directions

1. Pour vegetable oil into large skillet, and heat over medium-high heat.
2. Combine the flour, corn flour, and ice water in medium mixing bowl. Mix until soup-like.
3. Coat each piece of the vegetables, and place in the hot oil.
4. Cook for approximately 3 minutes, until golden brown. Remove from oil with tongs, and drain on a paper towel-covered plate.
5. Make additional batter as needed.

Hot and Sour Soup

Yield: 8–10 servings

Measure	Ingredients
8 c	Chicken broth
5 slices	Ginger root, fresh
1 tsp	Black peppercorns, whole
6	Green onions, chopped
1	Red bell pepper, diced
1 c	Mushrooms, fresh, sliced
½ c	Bamboo shoots
½ c	Rice vinegar
2 tsp	Chili powder
2 tsp	Sesame oil

Directions

1. In a large stockpot, heat broth, ginger root, and peppercorns. Bring to a boil. Reduce heat, and simmer for 20 minutes.

2. Strain broth, removing the peppercorns and ginger. Return strained broth to the stockpot.

3. Add onions, red bell pepper, mushrooms, bamboo shoots, vinegar, chili powder, and sesame oil.

4. Simmer 10 minutes, or until vegetables are tender.

5. Serve in bowls over rice.

Activity 11.10
Poster/Presentation—The Role of Geography and Asian Cuisine

Directions

China, Japan, and India together hold a large portion of the world's population, and each of those countries is home to a variety of culinary traditions. Explore how these customs and traditions began and how they are seen today, whether in modern restaurants or in the eating habits of the country. Select one country and research the practices that shaped the cuisine, cultural influences, and how that applies to modern life.

Create a three- to four-minute presentation that highlights this information. Be sure to include unique customs and practices, serving methods and styles, eating habits, and the role that geography played in the development of these customs and habits.

Take your notes in the space below. Use a separate sheet of paper, poster board, or your computer to create your presentation.

_____

_____

_____

_____

_____

_____

_____

_____

_____

_____

_____

_____

_____

_____

_____

_____

_____

_____

_____